Text By
WILLIAM HAFFORD

Photographs By
DAVID ELMS, JR. and JAMES TALLON

Maps By
W. RANDALL IRVINE

A summer showcase of sunflowers along U.S. Route 60 near Springerville. DAVID ELMS, JR.

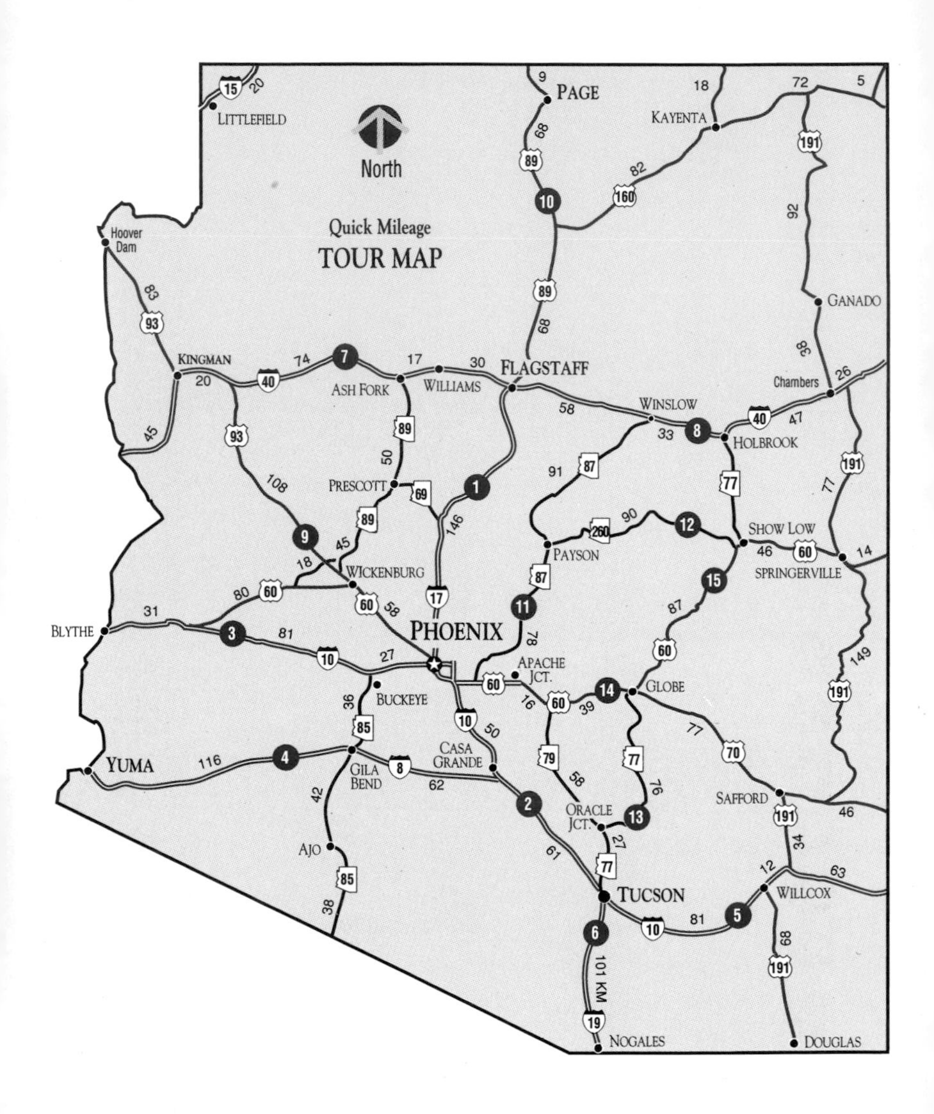

Prepared by the Book Division of *Arizona Highways* magazine, a monthly publication of the Arizona Department of Transportation.

Hugh Harelson — Publisher / Wesley Holden — Managing Editor
Gary Bennett — Creative Director / Melanie Johnston — Copy Editor
Cindy Mackey — Production Manager / Vicky Snow — Production Assistant.

Library of Congress Catalog Number 92-82725 ISBN 0-916179-38-9.

CONTENTS

With 113,909 square miles of stunning scenery, Arizona offers an almost limitless list of things to see and do. Yet, in this land of great space and distance, auto travelers anxious to move briskly from one scenic attraction to another sometimes put on mental blinders, lock their eyes on the center line, and zip down the highway toward a distant destination. Many motorists are unaware of the Arizona scenery, history, culture, and folklore along the state's major routes of travel.

This *Arizona Mileposts* travel guide is dedicated to providing the fast-moving motorist with travel commentary keyed to highway mileposts or interstate exits throughout the state. You will be able to pinpoint highlights along the way by relating them to corresponding milepost numbers or interstate exits. It's an easy, enlightening, and entertaining way to turn a routine trip into an interesting tour.

ARIZONA'S MILEPOST SYSTEM

MILE
0
0
0

Throughout the state, mileposts mark all interstate highways as well as U.S. and state routes. These vertical, green roadside signs, each with an appropriate number, appear on highway shoulders and are easily visible to passing motorists.

Mileposts ascend numerically from west to east and from south to north. Sometimes it may seem that milepost sequencing does not follow this format. For example, mileposts on U.S. Route 93 will descend numerically if you are traveling north from Phoenix to Lake Mead. But this is because

(Left) Caution. Antelope commonly graze the roadside areas through Petrified Forest National Park. See Tour 8, page 111, Exit 311 on Interstate 40. JAMES TALLON

the highway (even though it runs predominantly north/south within the state) enters Arizona on the state's western border near Hoover Dam, where its sequence starts.

Sometimes, when you change highways at junctions, or when one highway merges with another, you will notice a jump in sequencing. For example, assume you are traveling east on I-40 from the California border and you intend to head south from Flagstaff on I-17 to reach Phoenix. The mileposts on I-40 would ascend numerically to 195 where you would exit to I-17. The first milepost on I-17 would be 340, and from that point the mileposts would appear in descending order for the balance of your trip to Phoenix.

With the information above, following the milepost tour guide should be easy and informative. A statement at the beginning of each milepost tour chapter will indicate whether the milepost order is **ascending** or **descending**, and a notation will be provided in the text whenever there is a jump in sequencing due to a route change.

Milepost 228 — East of Superior on U.S. Route 60 engineers constructed a small tunnel along the steep sides of Queen Creek Canyon in 1922. Thirty years later they built the 1,149-foot multi-lane, lighted tunnel suitable for today's needs. DAVID ELMS, JR.

Purpose of the Milepost System

While the milepost system provides an excellent way to identify scenic and historic highlights, the system was initially developed to fulfill some practical objectives – mileposts are vital for fast response to highway emergencies. An accident reported with a milepost number enables highway patrol officers and medical personnel to pinpoint its location.

The Arizona Department of Transportation uses the milepost system to identify engineering, maintenance, and construction sites throughout the state. Whether it's a pot-hole marring the pavement or a flash flood that is sending torrents of water across a highway, mileposts offer a fast, efficient method for reporting and responding to problems.

Fifteen Easy-to-follow Milepost Tours

Designed primarily for motorists driving long distances on major highways, the *Arizona Mileposts* travel guide provides detailed tours on the 15 most-traveled routes in Arizona.

While the book can be effectively used by motorists entering the state at an Arizona border, all of the tours start from key junctions within the state. Milepost treks begin in Phoenix, Tucson, Flagstaff, Apache Junction, Globe, Payson, and Casa Grande. They proceed to destinations within the state or to the point where the highway crosses the Arizona border and enters a neighboring state.

Motorists traveling a given highway in a direction opposite that which is presented may simply go to the end of the tour chapter and follow the mileposts in reverse order. It is helpful to read about each upcoming milepost in advance so you'll have ample time to view it when you get there.

Driving Tips and Emergency Information

Arizona's rapid changes in altitude can quickly take you from desert sunshine to high-country snow. For information on road conditions, call (602) 252-1010, then enter the 4-digit category code 7623 when requested.

Highway emergencies can be reported to the Department of Public Safety by calling 1-800-525-5555. Emergency aid is much faster if you provide the nearest milepost number. If you are stalled on an Arizona highway, raise your hood to alert law enforcement officers and other travelers that you need help.

Safe Travel

The speed limit on interstate highways is 65 mph unless otherwise posted. Speed limits may vary on other highways. Arizona school zones are posted at 15 mph.

If a desert dust storm reduces visibility, turn on your headlights and proceed with caution, but do not lower your speed to a snail's pace, because (due to poor visibility) a following car might hit you. If poor visibility prevents you from proceeding safely, pull off the road to the right as far as possible. We emphasize "as far as possible." Stop and turn off your lights. Tragic pile-ups involving many vehicles have occurred in heavy dust storms.

Do not enter a roadway dip or desert wash during or after a heavy rainstorm until you have determined that the area is not flooded.

Make a mental note of roadside signs that provide information regarding first aid, hospitals, and communication stations.

Don't drive when drowsy. Pull into a roadside rest area or off the highway. Rest or walk for a few minutes.

Do not attempt to travel into back roads areas unless you are wilderness equipped and are carrying an ample supply of water. Before venturing into remote regions, tell someone your destination and planned date and time of return.

Seat belt use is mandatory in Arizona.

Littering Is Illegal

Please help Arizona preserve its spectacular scenery by keeping your trash with you until you can dispose of it in a proper container, such as those provided at Arizona roadside rest areas. Littering is punishable by a fine of up to $500.

Travel to Mexico

If you plan to drive in Mexico, you'll need Mexican auto insurance (obtainable at the border). In addition, if your car is financed, rented, or borrowed, you'll need a notarized letter of permission from the lien holder or owner to take the car into Mexico.

Should you plan to travel beyond the tourist zone near the border, each person in your vehicle will need a visa. They are obtained from the Mexican government at the border and require proof of citizenship (a passport, birth certificate, or voter's registration card). The larger border crossings are open around the clock. The smaller ones close between midnight and 8 A.M.

Additional Information

A wide variety of travel information may be obtained from the Arizona Office of Tourism, 1100 West Washington, Phoenix, AZ 85007. Telephone (602) 542-8687.

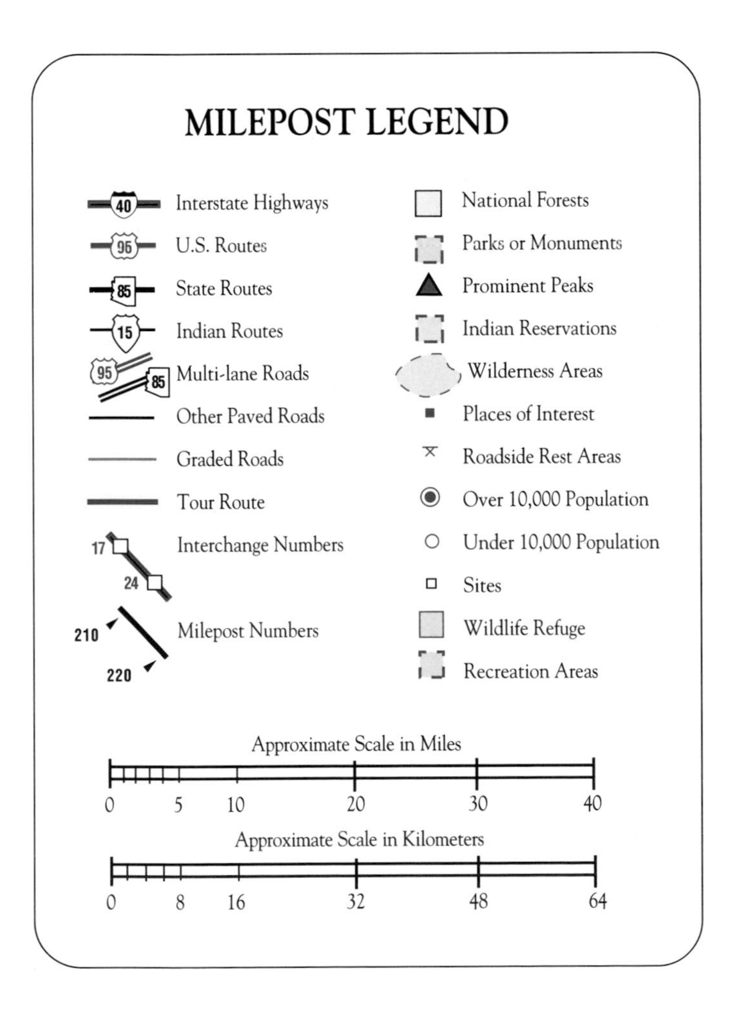

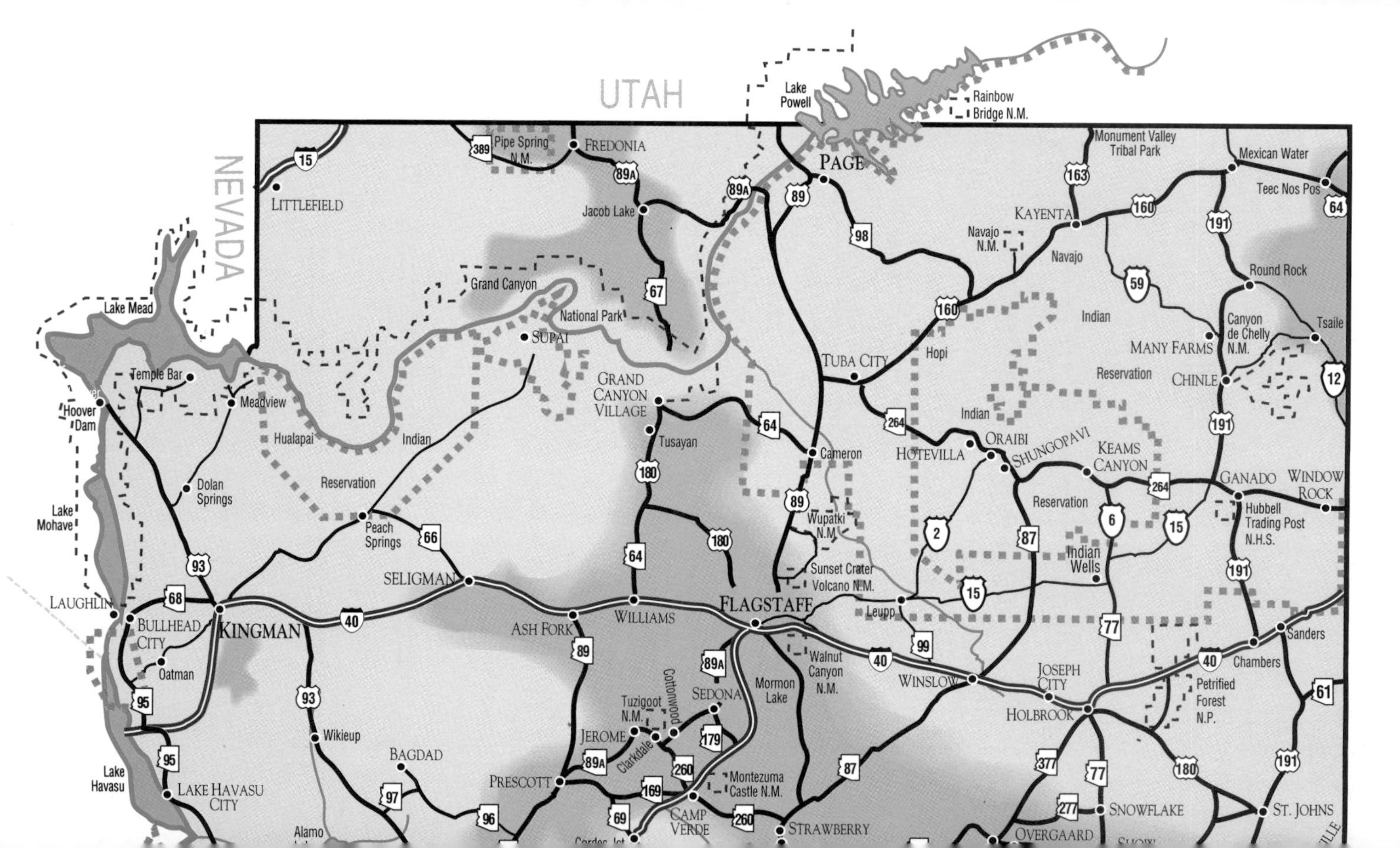
UTAH
NEVADA
Lake Powell
Rainbow Bridge N.M.
Pipe Spring N.M.
FREDONIA
PAGE
Monument Valley Tribal Park
Mexican Water
Teec Nos Pos
LITTLEFIELD
Jacob Lake
KAYENTA
Navajo N.M.
Navajo
Round Rock
Grand Canyon
National Park
SUPAI
Indian
Canyon de Chelly N.M.
Tsaile
Lake Mead
MANY FARMS
TUBA CITY
Hopi
Reservation
CHINLE
Temple Bar
Meadview
Hoover Dam
GRAND CANYON VILLAGE
Tusayan
Hualapai
Indian
Cameron
HOTEVILLA
ORAIBI
SHUNGOPAVI
KEAMS CANYON
GANADO
WINDOW ROCK
Dolan Springs
Reservation
Reservation
Hubbell Trading Post N.H.S.
Lake Mohave
Peach Springs
Wupatki N.M.
Indian Wells
SELIGMAN
Sunset Crater Volcano N.M.
LAUGHLIN
BULLHEAD CITY
KINGMAN
ASH FORK
WILLIAMS
FLAGSTAFF
Leupp
Sanders
Oatman
Walnut Canyon N.M.
Mormon Lake
WINSLOW
JOSEPH CITY
Chambers
Petrified Forest N.P.
Tuzigoot N.M.
Cottonwood
SEDONA
HOLBROOK
JEROME
Clarkdale
Wikieup
BAGDAD
Lake Havasu
PRESCOTT
Montezuma Castle N.M.
LAKE HAVASU CITY
CAMP VERDE
SNOWFLAKE
ST. JOHNS
Alamo
STRAWBERRY
OVERGAARD
15
389
89A
89
163
160
64
191
98
67
59
12
64
264
180
89
2
87
6
15
264
66
64
180
15
191
93
68
40
89
99
77
89A
40
61
95
93
179
260
87
377
77
180
191
95
97
96
89A
169
69
260
277

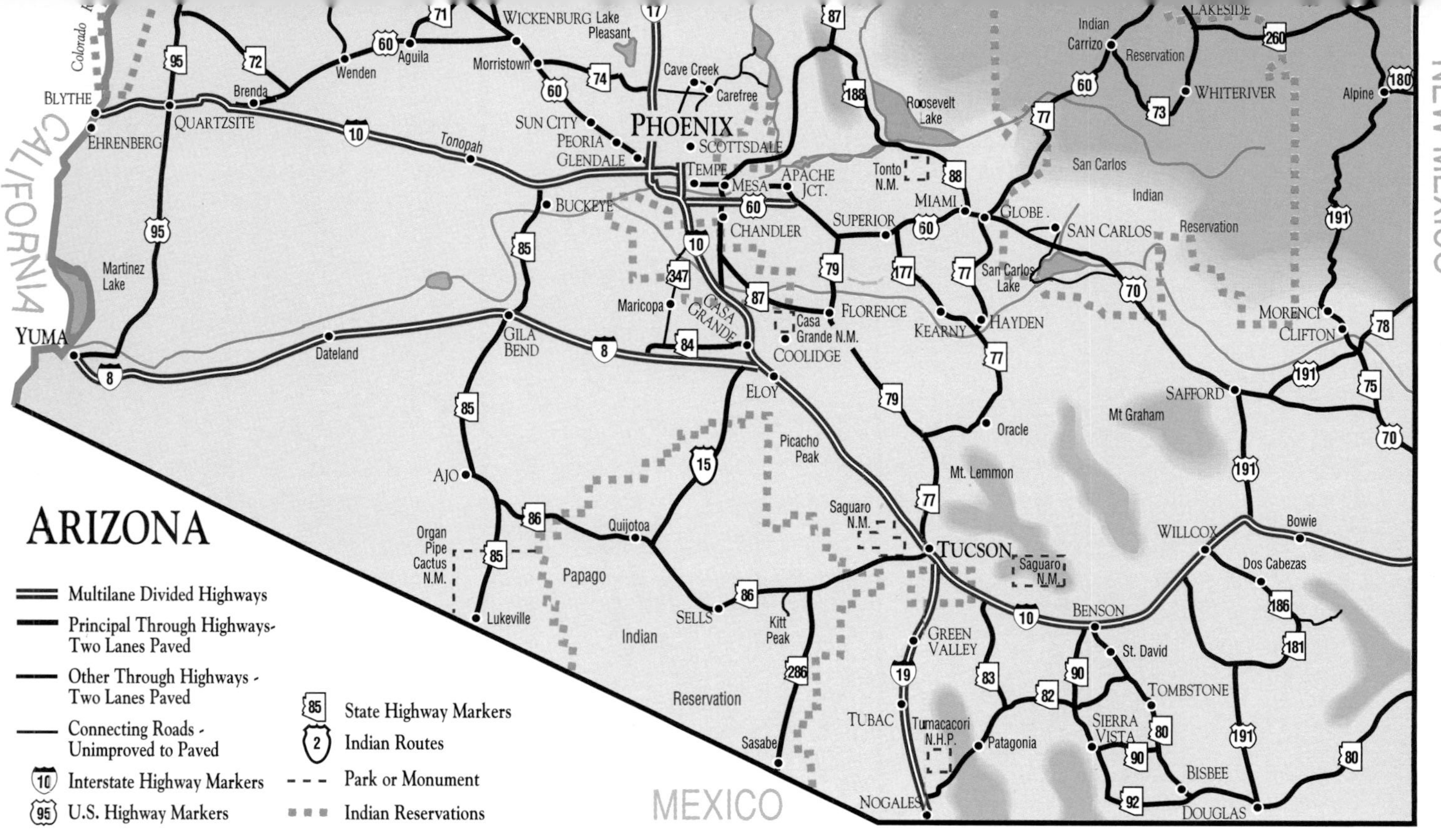

ARIZONA
NEW MEXICO
CALIFORNIA
MEXICO
Multilane Divided Highways
Principal Through Highways-Two Lanes Paved
Other Through Highways - Two Lanes Paved
Connecting Roads - Unimproved to Paved
Interstate Highway Markers
U.S. Highway Markers
State Highway Markers
Indian Routes
Park or Monument
Indian Reservations
PHOENIX
SCOTTSDALE
TEMPE
MESA
APACHE JCT.
CHANDLER
SUN CITY
PEORIA
GLENDALE
BUCKEYE
Cave Creek
Carefree
WICKENBURG
Lake Pleasant
Morristown
Wenden
Aguila
Brenda
QUARTZSITE
BLYTHE
EHRENBERG
Colorado
Tonopah
Martinez Lake
YUMA
Dateland
GILA BEND
Maricopa
CASA GRANDE
Casa Grande N.M.
COOLIDGE
FLORENCE
ELOY
Picacho Peak
SUPERIOR
MIAMI
GLOBE
SAN CARLOS
San Carlos Lake
KEARNY
HAYDEN
Tonto N.M.
Roosevelt Lake
Oracle
Mt. Lemmon
Saguaro N.M.
TUCSON
AJO
Organ Pipe Cactus N.M.
Lukeville
Papago
Indian
Reservation
Quijotoa
SELLS
Kitt Peak
Sasabe
GREEN VALLEY
TUBAC
Tumacacori N.H.P.
NOGALES
Patagonia
BENSON
St. David
TOMBSTONE
SIERRA VISTA
BISBEE
DOUGLAS
WILLCOX
Bowie
Dos Cabezas
SAFFORD
Mt Graham
MORENCI
CLIFTON
Alpine
LAKESIDE
WHITERIVER
Carrizo
San Carlos

TOUR PHOTOGRAPHS BY DAVID ELMS, JR.

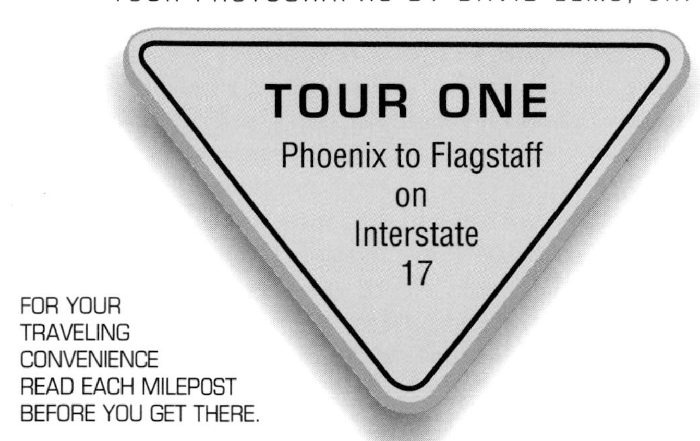

FOR YOUR TRAVELING CONVENIENCE READ EACH MILEPOST BEFORE YOU GET THERE.

Starting Point — Your journey starts in Phoenix, the state capital. For a brief profile of Phoenix, turn to page 27.

Along the Way—This 123-mile trip ascends nearly 6,000 feet. Your trek starts at about 1,100 feet above sea level in the lower Sonoran life zone where desert shrubs, saguaro cactus, and paloverde trees cover the flatlands and rugged desert hills. When you reach 4,000 feet the desert growth will give way to broad grassland and stands of juniper and piñon pine. Above 6,000 feet, thick upland forests of ponderosa pine start closing in on the highway. Near the end of the journey, a panoramic view of the San Francisco Mountains will visually take you to the highest point in Arizona, the 12,643-foot summit of Mount Humphreys.

En route, you will traverse wide stretches of rich grazing land, skirt rugged canyons where early mining camps boomed, and cross the route of the historic General Crook Trail. Scenic highlights include the soaring Bradshaw Mountains and the red rock country around Sedona. Side trips include a restored frontier fort, cliff dwellings of the prehistoric Sinagua people, and a reviving ghost town on the side of a steep mountain.

MILEPOST HIGHLIGHTS

Leaving Phoenix — Your tour starts on Interstate 17 as you approach the northern city limits of Phoenix. For a few miles, you will drive a relatively level stretch of highway, then start climbing. It is sometimes a good idea to shut off your air conditioner on the steepest hills. This helps prevent engine overheating.

(Left) Morning light on Montezuma Castle National Monument near Exit 289.

220 Central Arizona Project Aqueduct — Beyond this milepost, you will cross the CAP Aqueduct, a 335-mile-long canal that starts at the Colorado River on Arizona's western border and terminates southwest of Tucson. The CAP pumps water from the Colorado at 3,000 cubic feet per second and delivers nearly 2 billion gallons of water per day to the farms and communities of southern Arizona. The water flows through 14 pumping plants to raise it more than 2,000 feet in elevation from Lake Havasu to Tucson. The aqueduct has taken nearly 20 years to build and cost $2.5 billion. A number of related structures, such as storage, drainage, and distribution systems, are still under construction.

Exit 223 Ben Avery Shooting Range — Named for the Arizona outdoorsman and newspaperman instrumental in its founding, this shooting range lies just west of the highway. It hosts numerous national and international meets. The sprawling facility, rated as one of the nation's finest, offers a variety of ranges for rifle, pistol, skeet, and archery. The site, open to the public, also offers a 100-unit campground with RV hookups and showers. Cowboys originally named this area Biscuit Flat when a bag of biscuits developed a hole, leaving the cowpokes' lunch in a trail across the valley floor.

Exit 225 Pioneer Arizona Living History Museum — This frontier village, restored and furnished with historical accuracy, depicts life during the 1800s. You can walk the village (ride in a wagon on weekends), view exhibits, and watch craftsmen at work. There is a fee. Closed July through September.

227 Dead Man Wash — Most Arizona place names were assigned in the 1800s. In addition to Dead Man Wash, the state also has a Dead Man Canyon, Dead Man Creek, Dead Man Flat, Dead Man Gap, Dead Boy Point, and Dead River. This might lead you to conclude that frontier survival was difficult. It was.

227A Desert Hills Rest Area — This rest area includes ramadas, picnic tables, water, rest rooms, and a chance to observe Sonoran Desert vegetation close up. Plants growing in this area typify the lower Sonoran Desert, which makes up nearly one-third of Arizona's total land mass. Cactus here include saguaro, prickly pear, cholla, and barrel. The larger trees are mesquite (with rough dark bark) and paloverde (smooth bark, green limbs). Creosote bushes, usually under five feet in height, have tiny waxy, green leaves and a pungent fragrance when rubbed. A few leaves boiled in water make a bitter tea that some say is effective against cancer, colds, arthritis, poor circulation, and more. Ocotillo grow as clumps of upright sticks with sharp thorns and, after abundant spring rains, green leaves and cones of bright red flowers.

229 Gavilan Peak — Spanish for "hawk," this abruptly rising conical peak just off the highway to the northeast was the site of an 1870s battle between U.S. soldiers and Apaches who had raided a nearby ranch.

Exit 232 New River — The small settlement of New River, accessed at this exit, was the location of a crudely constructed stage station in the late 1860s. Its proprietor was Lord Darrell Duppa, a frontier character said to be a ne'er-do-well member of an aristocratic British family. If nothing else, Duppa was tenacious and protective of his property. It was said that he carried more than a half-dozen bullet scars acquired in skirmishes with marauding Apaches.

Exit 236 Ghost Town of Gillett — Table Mesa Road is another of Arizona's redundant place names. Table Mesa (*mesa* in Spanish means table) is the name of the flat-topped mountain to the east. To the west the ghost town of Gillett, on the banks of the Agua Fria River, milled the ore from a booming group of mines called Tip Top from 1875 to the mid-1890s. The road to this ghost town requires a trustworthy four-wheel-drive vehicle.

237 Bradshaw Mountains — To the northwest, the imposing Bradshaw Mountains rise to 7,950 feet. Named for

William Bradshaw, who first discovered silver in this region, the range was dotted with gold and silver mines and mining camps at the turn of the century. Today, most of the locations have become ghost towns or communities of summer homes.

243 **Approaching the Agua Fria River** — Translated from Spanish, the name means "cold water." Much of the year there is very little water, cold or otherwise, in the stream bed. But during infrequent heavy rains, the Agua Fria turns into a roaring torrent. About 20 miles to the southwest, Lake Pleasant stores the Agua Fria's waters. Soon these waters will mingle there with the waters of the Colorado River as the New Waddell Dam will enable Lake Pleasant to serve as a gigantic storage facility for the Central Arizona Project.

Exit 244 **Black Canyon City** — In the late 1800s a stage route from Phoenix to Prescott rambled through here and on up the canyon. In the northern end of 20-mile-long Black Canyon, the road was narrow and precipitous with few pullouts to allow another stage to pass. Drivers would pause at the beginnings of grades and give a blast on long tin horns. If another stage was approaching, that driver answered with a double blast and waited until the other stage passed. The canyon was the site of many stage robberies. Today, a growing residential community occupies the area. Black Canyon City has appeal for retired people and others who shun big cities.

Exit 248 **Old Mining Towns** — You are ascending Black Mesa, but this exit offers a scenic side trip for those who like old mining towns and dirt roads. Ghost towns, such as Bumble Bee

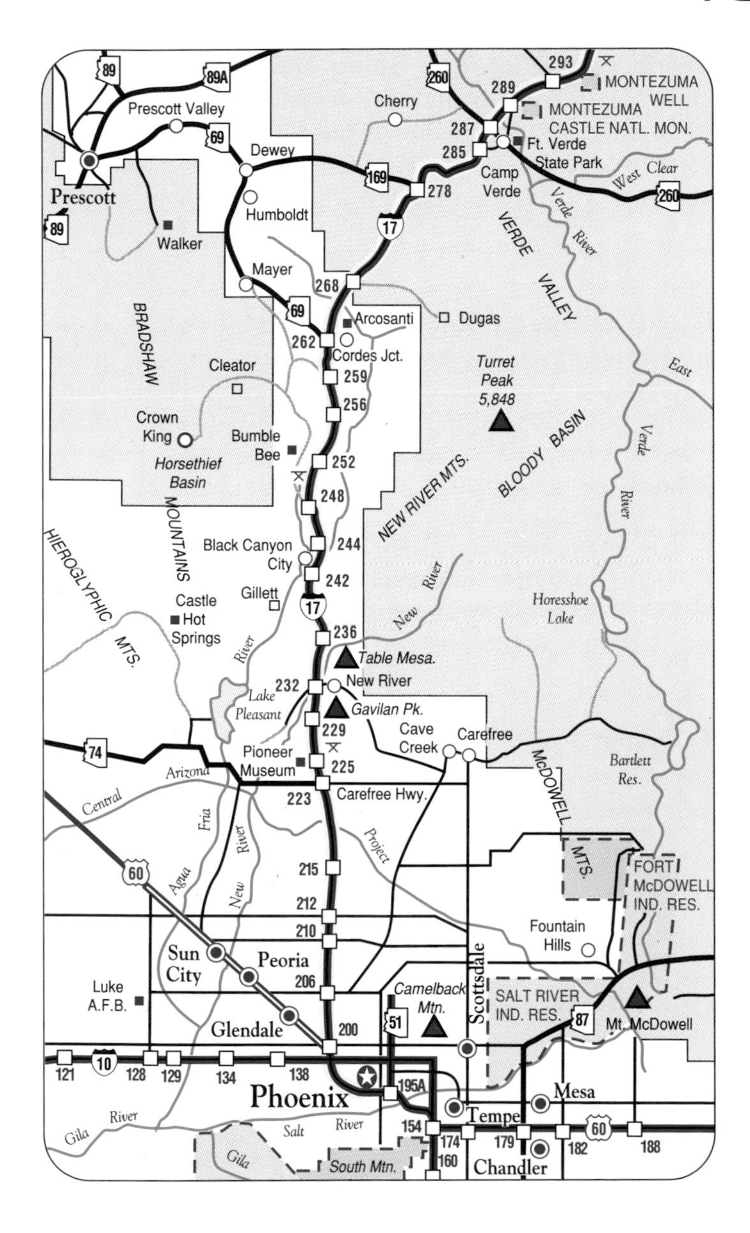

(6 miles down Black Canyon to the west) and Cleator, provide glimpses of Arizona's gold- and silver-mining past. Twenty-one zig-zag miles up the mountain from Bumble Bee, the once-thriving mining town of Crown King survives as a sleepy community of mountain homes served by a cafe and general store. About 7 miles southeast of Crown King, Horsethief Basin (a former hideout that justified its name) holds three Forest Service campgrounds with a total of 34 campsites.

249 The Last Saguaro Going North — Just before Milepost 250, the northbound lane enters a deep cut. Look to the hillside immediately west of the highway. The tall cactus with its arms upraised is the last saguaro on the route north. It also indicates that you are moving into a new geographic zone. Southbound travelers will see their first saguaros immediately south of Milepost 251.

Exit 252 Sunset Point Scenic Rest Area — Views of the rugged country to the west and the massive slopes of the Bradshaw Mountains make this award-winning roadside rest stop one of the more popular in Arizona. Facilities include ramadas, rest rooms, water, dump station, vending machines, and telephones. On busy holiday weekends free coffee is often available to weary travelers.

The late afternoon sun, casting long shadows from the highest ridges, makes the view especially spectacular. The tiny buildings at the bottom of the canyon are what is left of the stage station of Bumble Bee. It was so named in 1863 when prospectors found a beehive near the creek and were badly stung.

255 Turret Peak — About 15 miles to the east is Turret Peak (not visible from the highway). This was the site of a fierce 1873 engagement between the forces of Gen. George Crook and a band of renegade Tonto Apache that had tortured and killed three settlers near Wickenburg.

Arizona Historical Foundation

After 60 miles of hard riding they thought they had escaped safely. But at the head of Crook's troops was Alchesay, one of the most renowned government scouts on the frontier. Alchesay, in darkness, guided his scouts and U.S. soldiers to the top of Turret Peak where a lightning attack wiped out the outlaw band.

Alchesay was awarded the Congressional Medal of Honor for his heroics. He went on to serve as peacetime leader of his people, the White Mountain Apache, until his death in 1928.

Exit 259 Bloody Basin Road — The name begs for an explanation, but confusion obscures its source. Some believe Bloody Basin, about 10 miles to the southeast, got its name because of frequent Indian battles in the area. Others say the basin was a sheep trailway used in the semiannual drives between winter pasture in the desert and summer pasture in the high country. The story tells of a suspension bridge that collapsed, sending a herd of sheep to their bloody deaths in the basin below. This area is wild and remote and requires a high-clearance or four-wheel-drive vehicle.

Exit 262 **Cordes Junction and Arcosanti** — About 2.5 miles from Cordes Junction down a signed dirt road is Arcosanti, an ecologically-oriented community of the future. Italian architect Paolo Soleri has devoted more than 20 years to its creation. Although only partially complete, the site offers a guided tour of its unusual architecture (there is a fee), a gift shop, cafe, bakery, and free exhibits. (A drive-by view of Arcosanti is possible to the east of the interstate at Milepost 263.) Also at Exit 262, State Route 69 heads northwest 34 miles to Prescott, a delightful city of about 25,000 in pine-covered hills beyond the Bradshaw Mountains. President Abraham Lincoln ordered the establishment of Prescott as Arizona's territorial capital.

Exit 268 **Dugas and Orme Road** — In 1879, Fred Dugas decided to locate a ranch in the exact geographical center of Arizona. He missed the mark by a few miles, but the ranch (7 miles southeast of this exit) prospered and a U.S. Post Office was established there for a time. The exact geographical center of Arizona is approximately 6 miles east of this exit. Orme Road was named for a long-time Yavapai County ranching family.

276 **Dense Stands of Juniper** — Arizona has five species of juniper ranging from shrubby common juniper to massive alligator-bark juniper trees. Juniper is commonly used for fenceposts and firewood; the juniper berry provides oil of juniper used in patent medicines and to flavor gin.

Exit 278 **State Route 169** — The historic General Crook Trail parallels SR 169 and crosses Interstate 17 at this interchange. Established by Gen. George Crook in 1871, a crude wagon road ran southeast from the territorial capital at Prescott, 25 miles to the west, to remote Fort Apache in the White Mountains. Parts of the trail are still visible and marked with rock cairns. A century ago this route was an important transportation avenue for troops and supplies.

The small residential area of Cherry, northwest of this exit, takes its name from wild cherry trees growing along the creek.

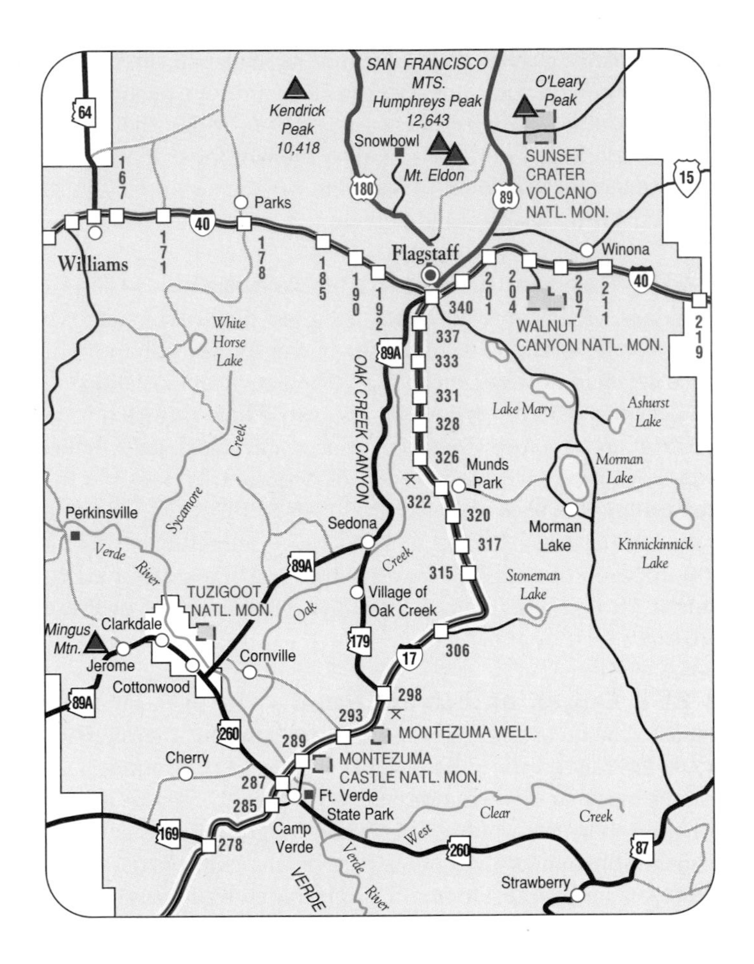

281 Descent to Verde Valley — At this point, you start descending through Copper Canyon to the broad valley of the Verde River. The General Crook Trail, continuing toward the east, ran along the bottom of this canyon, which was considered safe haven because the Indians, for unknown reasons, would not enter it. At Milepost 283, look toward the distant horizon at an approximate 2 o'clock position. A visible notch is the point where Crook's trail ascended to the high country and went east along the precipitous Mogollon Rim.

284 Oak Creek Canyon — The view to the north includes your first glimpse of the spectacular red rock cliffs of Oak Creek Canyon, with the San Francisco Peaks rising in the distance.

Exit 285 Camp Verde — Camp Lincoln was established in 1864 to protect white settlers and miners from Yavapai and

Apache Indians whose homeland the settlers had invaded. Camp Lincoln became Camp Verde and in 1868, Fort Verde. The community retained the name Camp Verde. Today, Fort Verde State Historic Park, 2 miles east of this exit, offers a restored version of the outpost built in 1871. A modest fee is charged.

Exit 287 **Tuzigoot National Monument** — State Route 260 provides a popular 25-mile (each way) side trip through the Verde Valley to Dead Horse Ranch State Park, a popular camping and fishing spot on the banks of the Verde River; Tuzigoot National Monument, prehistoric Indian dwellings near the old smelter town of Clarkdale; and the lively ghost town of Jerome. Perched on the steep sides of Mingus Mountain, Jerome offers art galleries, craft shops, restaurants, and the old buildings of a once-prosperous copper mining town.

Exit 288 **Verde River** — This small but reliable river starts in Chino Valley, about 50 miles to the northwest, and flows southeast until it joins the Salt River east of Phoenix. The Verde was so named by early explorers for the color of its water as it reflected the vegetation along its banks.

Exit 289 **Montezuma Castle National Monument** — Two miles east of this exit, Sinagua Indians built (circa A.D. 1200) a towering, five-story cliff dwelling in a limestone alcove nearly 100 feet above Beaver Creek. The impressive ruins, misnamed during frontier days, were never a part of Montezuma's Aztec empire. There is a visitor center with a variety of exhibits. A tree-shaded picnic area is situated near the creek. Modest entry fee.

Exit 293 **Montezuma Well** — This oasis, created by fresh-water springs, is a part of Montezuma Castle National Monument. The site features a small lake in a sinkhole (475 feet across) where early Sinagua Indians built rock pueblos. The water, which flows at more than 1,000 gallons per minute, was used by prehistoric inhabitants to irrigate crops. Modern farmers use the water and some of the same canals. Five miles east of I-17. No fee.

296 Rest Area — A roadside stop with ramadas, picnic tables, water, and rest rooms is located beyond this milepost. Views from the rest area include the imposing red rock formations in the Sedona area to the north.

Exit 298 Junction of State Route 179 — Twelve miles northwest on Route 179, the resort and leisure-living community of Sedona nestles among towering, erosion-carved red sandstone buttes and cliffs. Famous for its art galleries, craft shops, and fine restaurants, Sedona also serves as a gateway to the magnificent scenery of Oak Creek Canyon.

Exit 306 Stoneman Lake — Ten miles to the east lies one of Arizona's few natural lakes. Rain and snowmelt fill the basin of this extinct volcano. Arizona Army wife Martha Summerhayes wrote of her arduous wagon trip through the area in 1875, "It was good to our tired eyes, which had gazed upon nothing but burnt rocks and alkali plains for so many days. Our camp was beautiful beyond description, and lay near the edge of the mesa, whence we could look down upon the lovely lake."

310 Ponderosa Pine Forest — This milepost, at 6,100 feet elevation, marks the beginning of a huge ponderosa pine forest that stretches southeast all the way to the New Mexico border and beyond. On the ridge directly ahead, you can see the first ponderosa pines on this northerly route. In less than 4 miles the forest giants will surround you.

319 San Francisco Mountains — This milepost presents a good view of the San Francisco Mountains and the highest point in Arizona, 12,643-foot Humphreys Peak. Created by volcanic eruptions nearly 2.8 million years ago, the higher peaks are usually covered with snow from fall through late spring. The slopes of the Snowbowl attract skiers from thoughout the U.S.

Exit 320 Schnebly Hill Road — Named for the founding family of the town of Sedona, the dirt road to the west winds about 7 miles through thick woods to a vista point that looks down on the spectacular scenery of Oak Creek Canyon and Sedona's red rock country. In pioneer days this route was used to travel to Flagstaff for supplies. In good weather the narrow dirt road can be driven another 6 miles to Sedona. It's a memorable ride, but hairpin turns and treacherously steep drop-offs cause butterflies for many travelers. The road is closed during winter.

Exit 322 Munds Park — Named for James Mund, who homesteaded and raised stock in the area, this broad mountain meadow has evolved into a small community with a motel, restaurants, service stations, and a golf course. The road to the east (paved for a short distance) leads 12 miles to Mormon Lake and a series of other small, high-country lakes offering good fishing, numerous campgrounds, and gorgeous scenery.

323 Christensen Rest Area — North of this milepost you'll find a welcoming roadside rest area ideal for a picnic. The site offers ramadas, tables, water, rest rooms, and telephones.

340 Flagstaff, Interstate 17 Ends — At this point, Interstate 17 ends at a junction with Interstate 40, which runs 475 miles west to Los Angeles and 327 miles east to Albuquerque. For more information on the Flagstaff area see page 131.

TOUR PHOTOGRAPHS BY JAMES TALLON

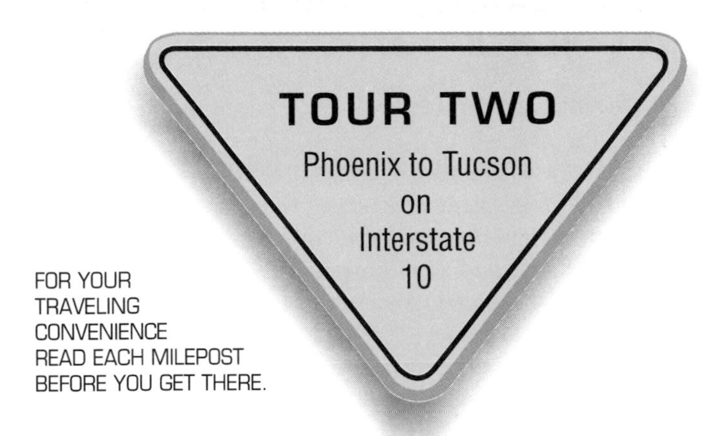

FOR YOUR TRAVELING CONVENIENCE READ EACH MILEPOST BEFORE YOU GET THERE.

Starting Point — This tour starts in Phoenix, state capital of Arizona. About 2,000 years ago, migrating Indians from Mexico established a community in the area of present-day Phoenix. Known today as the Hohokam ("the vanished ones" in the Pima Indian language), they engineered an extensive canal system, grew corn, beans, melons, and cotton, made pottery, wove baskets, created sophisticated jewelry, and thrived in the warm climate. About A.D. 1350 they disappeared. No one is sure why.

More than 500 years later, a new city began to take form on the site of the old Hohokam settlements. One of the better-educated early settlers, Lord Darrell Duppa (see p.17, Exit 232) observed, "A new city will spring phoenix-like upon the ruins of a former civilization." Today, Phoenix ranks among the nation's 10 largest cities.

The warm climate and numerous resorts are big attractions for visitors. Permanent residents prize the area for its mild winters and a central location that provides easy access to Arizona's spectacular scenery and outdoor recreational sites.

Along the Way — As you travel southeast toward Tucson, interstate exit numbers are in ascending order. The topography displays rugged hills, impressive desert mountain ranges, and the varied plant life of the Sonoran Desert. You will see giant saguaro cactus and have the opportunity to visit prehistoric Indian ruins many believe housed an ancient astronomical observatory. You will pass the remains of an old volcanic peak where Arizona's only Civil War battle was fought, then approach Tucson in the shadow of the 9,157-foot Santa Catalina Mountains.

(Left) East of Exit 185, four-story Casa Grande Ruins National Monument is believed to have been an astronomical observatory for the ancient Hohokam.

MILEPOST HIGHLIGHTS

Superstition Freeway — We begin this tour where the divided U.S. Route 60, called the Superstition Freeway, heads toward the distant wild canyons of the Superstition Mountains, 30 miles to the east. This notorious range, formed by erosion of an ancient volcanic dome and sometimes called "the slag heaps of hell," is the purported location of the legendary Lost Dutchman gold mine.

The legend centers around prospector Jacob Waltz. In the latter part of the 1800s "the Dutchman," as he was called, would occasionally emerge from the Superstitions with gold nuggets. Supposedly he had found the old Peralta mine that had been part of the original land grant from Spain. Since Waltz's death in the early 1890s, many people have lost their lives or just "vanished" while searching for the Lost Dutchman Mine.

For a distant view of the Superstitions, look to the east as you pass Exit 155.

Exit 157 **South Mountain Park** — The world's largest city park (nearly 17,000 acres) encompasses South Mountain, a scenic desert mountain range featuring numerous picnic ramadas and miles of hiking trails. A scenic drive up the mountain's north slope to the summit starts on south Central Avenue.

161 **Gila River Indian Reservation** — South of this milepost, you will enter a 37,200-acre reservation for the Pima and Maricopa Indian tribes, primarily agricultural people. Tribal headquarters are located at Sacaton, 8 miles southeast of Interstate 10 at Exit 175.

Directly to the west, and running through a sector of the reservation, are the sharp-ridged Estrella ("star" in Spanish) Mountains. This waterless range with steep, rock-strewn canyons is home to many species of desert wildlife, including a herd of desert bighorn sheep.

Exit 162B **Firebird International Raceway** — This man-made lake and race track facility just to the west offers a

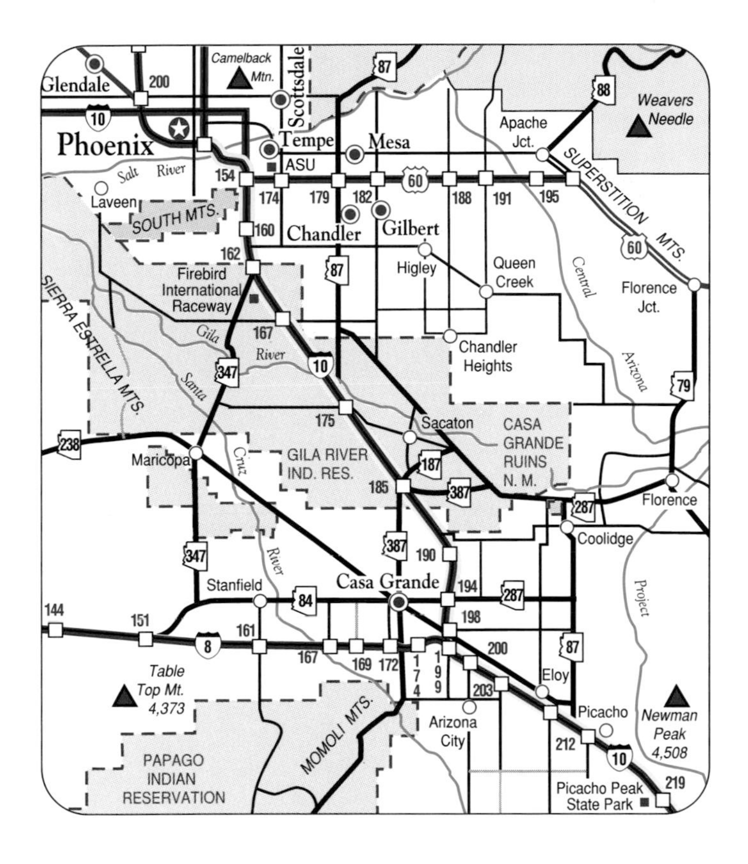

year-round schedule of automobile and speedboat racing events. Included is the International Hot Boat Association Finals where sleek water craft reach speeds of more than 220 miles per hour.

169 Flora of the Sonoran Desert — You are now entering an area that richly displays the plant life of the lower Sonoran Desert. Prickly pear, cholla, and barrel cactus thrive in this harsh land. About 3 miles to the south, you will encounter a large stand of saguaro cactus. Plant life also includes creosote, a bush usually under five feet in height with small, waxy green leaves. The pungent fragrance of the plant is most noticeable after desert rainstorms. Ocotillo present a cluster of tall sticks with thorns and are sometimes tipped with bright red-orange flowers in spring. The large, low-growing trees are either mesquite or paloverde. Paloverde, which means "green stick" in Spanish, exhibit green bark and limbs. Mesquite trees have a dark, rough bark. Beans from the mesquite were a primary food source for early inhabitants.

171 Saguaro Cactus — Just beyond this milepost, in the rocky hills along the highway, you will see large stands of saguaros. Often living beyond 200 years, they can soar to heights of 50 feet. The creamy white blossom of the saguaro is Arizona's state flower.

173 Gila River — Just south of this milepost, you'll cross the Gila River. The Gila starts in the high mountain country of New Mexico, then winds westerly across Arizona to join the Colorado River at the state's western boundary. In the early years of this century, a portion of the lower Gila near its confluence with the Colorado River could be traveled by small boat. Today, Coolidge Dam, 80 miles east of here, impounds the waters of the Gila. Most of the time the river is dry below that point. Prior to 1853, the Gila marked the southern boundary of Arizona, with everything to the south belonging to Mexico. The United States bought the 45,500 square miles of southern Arizona for $10 million under the Gadsden Purchase.

Exit 175 Gila Arts and Crafts Center — A half mile to the west is the Indian village of Bapchule and the Gila Arts and Crafts Center. A modern building of Indian architectural design, the center features a Native American historical museum, a coffee shop, and a gift shop that offers jewelry, pottery, baskets, and other crafts from numerous Indian tribes of the Southwest. Open daily; admission free.

177 Agriculture — The extensive cultivated areas here belong to Indian farmers on the Gila River Indian Reservation. This land, together with the thousands of rich, irrigated acres beyond the boundaries of the reservation, comprises one of Arizona's major farming regions, where cotton has long been a primary crop.

181 Rest Area — Beyond this milepost is an exit that leads to a rest area with ramadas, picnic tables, and rest rooms.

Exit 185 Casa Grande Ruins National Monument — To visit one of the Southwest's most intriguing ruins, exit here, then proceed east on State Route 387 14 miles to the monument. The trip takes you through the Sacaton Mountains where slopes are covered with formations of eroded granite boulders. In the spring, bright wildflowers carpet the hills.

The massive adobe ruins at Casa Grande were abandoned about A.D. 1350 by Hohokam Indians. The four-story structure may have served as an astronomical observatory with ceremonial chambers. Open daily; a modest fee is charged.

This same exit, taken to the south, leads to the community of Casa Grande, an agricultural center (pop. 20,000) that provides full services for travelers. Just beyond Exit 185, you leave the Gila River Indian Reservation.

Exit 199 Junction of Interstates 10 and 8 — Interstate 8 begins here and crosses southwestern Arizona, leaving the state at the Colorado River near Yuma. The route continues west to end at San Diego. A milepost tour beginning at this point (Exit 199) and continuing west on Interstate 8 to the Arizona border, is profiled in Chapter 4, beginning on page 49.

Exit 203 Eloy and Picacho Peak — The town of Eloy, accessed by this exit, started out as a lonely Southern Pacific Railroad section house in the early 20th century. The name, it is said, came about when a railroader took one look at the area and exclaimed "Eloi!," supposedly Spanish for the Biblical "Eli, Lama

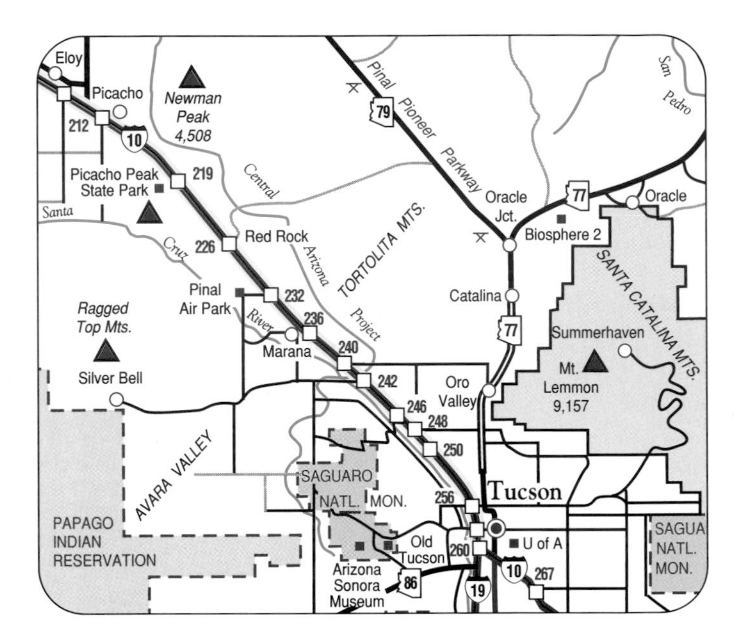

Sabachthani?" or, "My God, why hast Thou forsaken me?" But the loneliness dissipated as cotton farmers moved into the area and Eloy began to grow into a substantial community. The distant sharp peak extending above the horizon dead ahead is Picacho Peak, site of the only Arizona Civil War skirmish.

210 Pecan Groves — Notice the extensive groves of pecan trees. Abundant irrigation water is all that is required for these native American trees to flourish in the desert climate. Each year, more than a million pounds of pecans are produced at this 900-acre site.

Exit 212 Picacho — On the northeast side of the interstate stands the business area of the small roadside community of Picacho, Spanish for "peak." In an earlier era of automobile travel — when the journey across the desert was slow — Picacho was an important way station between Tucson and Phoenix. Today, with a divided freeway, most vehicles speed on by.

214 Picacho Mountains — Northeast of the highway are the Picacho Mountains whose highest point is 4,508-foot Newman Peak. Notice the distinct, man-made line running just above the base of the range. This is the Central Arizona Project Aqueduct, which transports millions of gallons of water from the Colorado River (nearly 200 air-miles away) to the towns, farms, and Indian reservations of southern Arizona.

216 Rest Area — Beyond this milepost is an exit to a roadside rest area with ramadas, picnic tables, and rest rooms.

Exit 219 Picacho Peak State Park — In frontier days, the towering volcanic remains of the redundantly named Picacho Peak served as a beacon for travelers. (*Picachio* means "peak" in Spanish). The pass between the peak and the Picacho Mountains was a busy avenue of travel; the Butterfield Overland Stage Line established a station not far from the peak in the 1850s.

The westernmost conflict of the Civil War was fought near Picacho Peak in 1862. Three men were killed and five wounded in the brief skirmish between Capt. Sherod Hunter's Confederate troops and Col. James Carleton's California column.

Picacho Peak State Park, about a half-mile off the road at this exit, offers picnic areas, a campground, showers, hookups, and numerous hiking trails. Experienced hikers sometimes climb to the summit of the 3,382-foot peak. Modest fees are charged for camping and day use.

Exit 226 Red Rock — Named for the red butte northeast of the highway, Red Rock was an important rail stop and the headquarters of an extensive ranching operation in the 1800s. The Aguirre Cattle Company, established in 1892 by a Mexican family that traced its New World lineage back to the days of the conquistadors, ran thousands of cattle in this area. All that remains of Red Rock is a railroad water tank, just off the freeway. However, the Aguirre Cattle Company still prospers.

229 Pinal Airpark — To the southwest of the interstate, this retired World War II auxiliary air field in the dry desert is ideal for storing fleets of large jet aircraft. While surplus planes from airlines are mothballed here, others are being restored, repainted, and returned to service. Sorry, no visitors allowed.

Exit 236 Marana — Marana, Spanish for "thicket," refers to the jungle of mesquite and catclaw that once grew here. This is the location of a University of Arizona agricultural center and is an important community in this broad farming region. As you reach the crest of the overpass, take note of a cotton gin just off the freeway. In the picking season, hundreds of new bales of cotton stand in the yard around the gin.

240 Limestone Quarry and Cement Plant — Southwest of the highway, in a set of hills known as Picacho de Calera, Spanish for "limestone quarry," you see a terraced area. A 5-mile conveyor belt, one of the longest in the United States, transports the limestone to the huge Arizona Portland Cement Company plant located beyond Milepost 242. The facility can produce more than a million tons of cement each year.

246 Santa Catalina Mountains — At the crest of the overpass just south of this milepost, look to the northeast for an unobstructed view of the forest-topped Santa Catalina Mountains. Mt. Lemmon, the tip of an immense granite core that formed perhaps 1.5 billion years ago, is the highest point in this range, at 9,157 feet. Ski slopes here are the southernmost in the United States and just an hour's drive from the city of Tucson. An astronomical observatory also operates on the peak.

Exit 257 Speedway Boulevard — The University of Arizona is about 2 miles east on Speedway Boulevard. Founded in 1891 with a single building in an undeveloped desert setting, the institution now enrolls nearly 40,000 students. Ten miles to the west in the Tucson Mountains is the internationally acclaimed Arizona-Sonora Desert Museum, the western segment of the Saguaro National Monument, and Old Tucson Studios, a frontier amusement park created from old Western-movie sets.

Exit 257A Tucson's Historic Walking Tour — Take the St. Mary's Road exit to nearly 30 points of interest on this self-guided tour of the Old Pueblo's historic downtown. You may obtain a tour map at the Tucson Chamber of Commerce, 465 West St. Mary's Road (792-1212). For more information on Tucson, turn to page 77.

The Phoenix to Tucson milepost tour ends here. If you are continuing east on Interstate 10, a milepost tour for that route is profiled in Chapter 5, page 65. If you intend to drive south on Interstate 19 to Nogales and the Mexican border, turn to the milepost trip in Chapter 6, page 77.

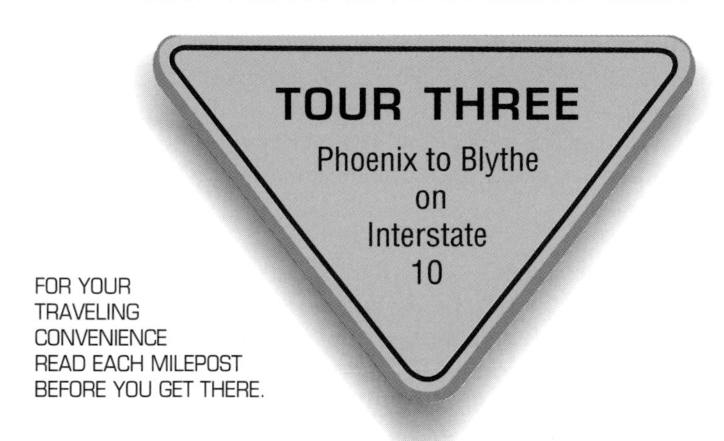

FOR YOUR TRAVELING CONVENIENCE READ EACH MILEPOST BEFORE YOU GET THERE.

Starting Point — Your tour starts in Phoenix, the state capital of Arizona. For a brief profile of Phoenix, turn to page 27.

Along the Way — From the palm-lined thoroughfares of Phoenix, you will head west through a lush agricultural area, then cross more than 120 miles of starkly beautiful but inhospitable desert. Even today, the land between Arizona's capital city and the Colorado River is largely unsettled. It is a land of arid plains and wildly convoluted mountains where only the hardiest plants and animals can survive.

MILEPOST HIGHLIGHTS

Note: Mileposts on this tour will appear in descending order as you drive west toward the California border.

MILE 135 **Western City Limits of Phoenix** — At this milepost, you will cross the western boundary of the city of Phoenix and pass through, or near, Tolleson, Avondale, Goodyear, and Litchfield Park. All are either support communities for the vast agricultural district that surrounds them or bedroom communities of Phoenix.

133 **Estrella Mountains** — The incline just ahead provides a good view of the Estrella Mountains to the south. This waterless range, with steep, rocky canyons, is home for many species of desert wildlife, including desert bighorn sheep. The Butterfield Stage once ran just south of the Estrellas.

(Left) West of Phoenix, the Interstate passes through a large agricultural area. This irrigated cotton field is south of Milepost 132.

132 Cultivated Fields — At this point, you are surrounded by more than 200,000 acres of rich desert farmland where cotton is one of the leading crops. With an annual rainfall of less than eight inches, this major agricultural region depends almost entirely on irrigation water impounded behind dams or drawn from deep wells.

131 Agua Fria River — Beyond this milepost, you will cross the dry stream bed of the Agua Fria (Spanish for "cold water") River, which rises more than 100 miles north of here between Prescott and Mingus Mountain. Its width indicates the river's capacity for violent flooding during runoff periods. A dam at Lake Pleasant, 30 miles upstream, now holds back the river, so water rarely flows at this point.

128 Litchfield Park and Goodyear — During World War I the nation's supply of Egyptian cotton, critical in the wartime manufacture of tires, was cut off by the German blockade. So, in 1916, the Goodyear Tire and Rubber Company purchased land in this area and began growing long-fibered cotton. The community to the immediate south housed the workers and assumed the name Goodyear, while the town just to the north, built to house management, was named for the company executive Paul Litchfield.

127 Luke Air Force Base — About 5 miles north of this milepost lies one of the nation's major military air bases. Vastly expanded during World War II, the facility is named for famed World War I Arizona air ace, Frank Luke, Jr. In his brief 30-day combat career, Luke, known as the "Balloon Buster," downed 21 enemy aircraft before dying in action. Posthumously, he was awarded the Congressional Medal of Honor.

125 Phoenix Trotting Park — The imposing empty structure to the south was built in the mid-1960s as a track for harness racing, complete with a glass-enclosed, air-conditioned grandstand. The silks-and-sulky set didn't go over too well, so after a few seasons the park closed.

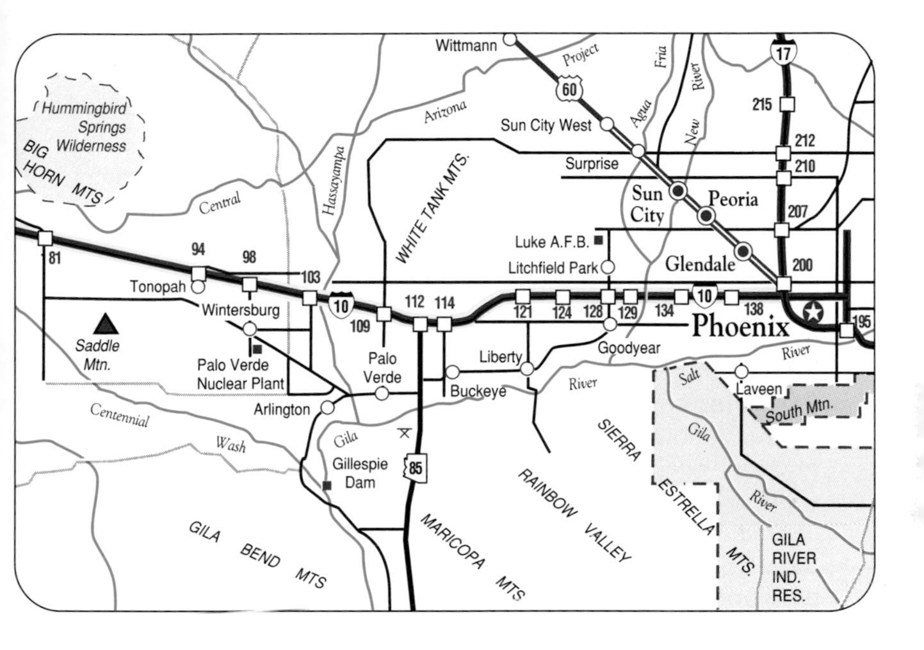

122 White Tank Mountains — These rugged mountains, seen several miles to the northwest, are composed of a core of Precambrian rock between one- and two-billion years old. For countless centuries, water spilling off a cliff in the mountains carved deep natural tanks into a slope of whitish rock, hence the name White Tank Mountains. More than 90 years ago, a cloudburst loosened the land, causing a section of the mountain to collapse and fill in one of the larger tanks. Ancient man left hundreds of petroglyphs to record his presence. Much of the White Tank range is protected as a Maricopa County park.

120 Flood Control Dikes — To the north, at about 2 o'clock, you'll see a long, man-made line of earth. This is one of a series of dikes built in this region to hold back flood waters. Infrequent rain in the desert often arrives as a sudden deluge that can cause great damage if uncontrolled. As you proceed west, the dikes will become more apparent.

118 Creosote Bushes — These low-growing shrubs with dull-green leaves thrive in the most arid regions. Stretching across the desert on both sides of the highway, they will continue in abundance as you proceed west. Creosote plants may be the oldest living things on earth. Scientists judge some specimens to be nearly 12,000 years old. A central plant sends out runners that pop up as extensions. These send out more runners, and more extensions shoot up. This process can go on for many centuries. Other plants seen in the area include saguaro, cholla, and barrel cactus, and paloverde and ironwood trees.

Exit 112 **Junction with State Route 85** — The paved highway heading south from this exit intersects with Interstate 8 near the community of Gila Bend. Interstate 8 starts in Casa Grande, branching west from Interstate 10, and extends through Yuma and on to San Diego. A tour of State Route 85 and Interstate 8 begins on page 52.

105 **Hassayampa River** — When water flows in this river, most of it flows underground. *Hassayampa* is an Indian term said to mean "river running upside down." During the frontier era, some rich gold and silver strikes were made along its course. This excitement caused many prospectors to exaggerate the value of their claims, many of which were worthless. A legend finally developed that anyone who drinks from the Hassayampa never utters a word of truth.

101 **Palo Verde Nuclear Generating Station** — Looking directly south, you have a clear view of the buff-colored domes of the nation's largest producer of nuclear-generated electricity. The Palo Verde Nuclear Generating Station (capacity 3,810 megawatts) serves nearly four million residents in Arizona, California, New Mexico, and Texas. You may visit the facility's Energy Information Center without a reservation, Monday through Friday (go south at Exit 98).

91 **Palo Verde Hills and Saddle Mountain** — The dark, smoothly contoured formations of the Palo Verde Hills, named for the profusion of paloverde trees in the area, rise

directly south of the highway. Also south of the highway appears the ragged form of Saddle Mountain (also called Saddle Back Mountain). Although decidedly different in appearance, both are primarily of volcanic composition. About 14 miles farther west, look back to see why Saddle Mountain was given its name.

88 **Big Horn Mountains** — These rugged mountains, directly north, are named for herds of desert bighorn sheep that roamed the area in frontier times. Like many mountains in the region, the Big Horn range is formed mostly of volcanic material. Components include lava, compacted volcanic ash, and large rock fragments cemented together with lava or ash. Taken as a whole, this combination results in extremely forbidding terrain.

87 **Burnt Well Rest Area** — Beyond this milepost is a large rest area with ramadas, tables, rest rooms, water, and a pet exercise area. A fire ran through the region and burned away the grass and brush around a nearby watering station on the Harquahala Plain, hence the name Burnt Well. If you walk north into the desert a short distance you can see a light-colored, man-made line at the base of the Big Horn Mountains. The line indicates the route of the 330-mile-long Central Arizona Project Aqueduct, which can carry nearly 2 billion gallons of water per day from the Colorado River to the farms and communities of southern Arizona.

82 **Eagle Tail Mountains** — The jagged mountains southwest of the highway at a 10 o'clock position received their name because they exhibit a pair of distinct stone spires

resembling the plumes of an eagle's tail. The ones that inspired the name are not visible from the highway.

81 Harquahala Mountains — North, at a 2 o'clock position, are the Harquahala (Mohave Indian for "water high up") Mountains. In 1920, the Smithsonian Institution sponsored a solar observatory near the summit of Harquahala Peak (5,600 feet). The location was ideal for solar radiation studies, but supplying the site was so difficult that the facility was closed after five years of operation. Today, the weathered remains of the observatory are protected by the Bureau of Land Management.

78 Courthouse Rock — At a 10 o'clock position, out from the base of the Eagle Tail Mountains, stands the impressive bulk of Courthouse Rock. Some say the name comes from the shape of the rock; others tell the story that near here the Clantons (same family that had the shoot-out with Wyatt Earp at the OK Corral) caught up with rustlers who had taken some cattle the Clantons had previously rustled from someone else. Before dispatching the captives to the "big ranch in the sky," a brief and informal trial was held.

77 Saddle Mountain — Pull off the highway and look back toward Saddle Mountain. The immense concavity (or saddle) in the outline of the mountain explains its name.

67 Central Arizona Project Aqueduct — Near this milepost and at several locations farther west, you will cross the meandering path of the CAP. The canal changes course in an attempt to maintain gravity flow as much as possible. Even so, pump stations are required at various points to lift the water from 700 feet at Colorado River level, to 1,300 feet near Phoenix, and 2,400 feet near Tucson.

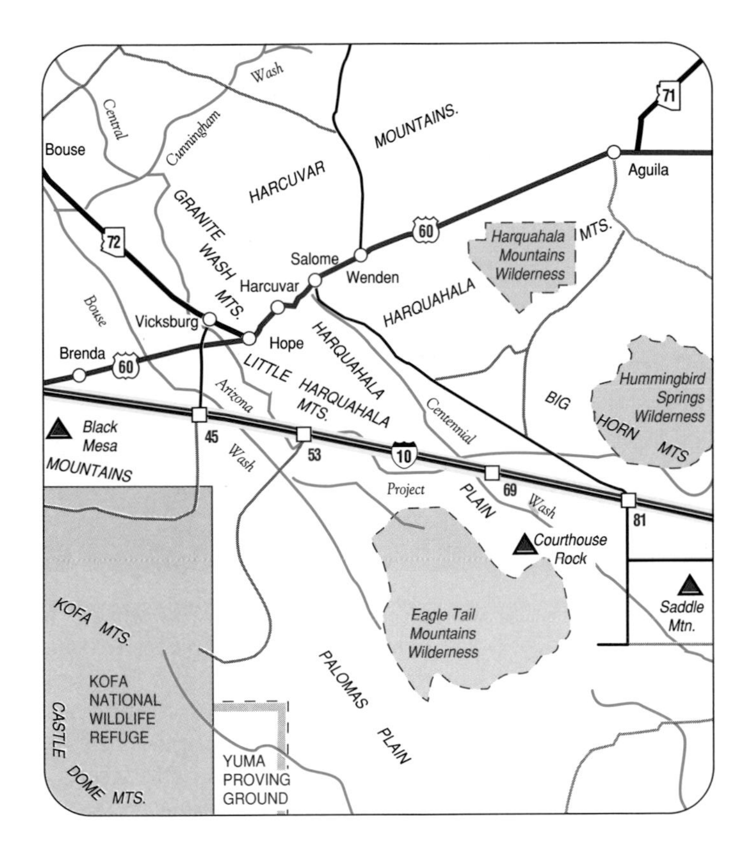

Exit 53 Rest Area — West of this exit is the Bouse Wash roadside rest area with ramadas, tables, rest rooms, water, pay telephone, and vending machines.

Exit 45 Vicksburg Road — Vicksburg was named for Victor Satterdahl, who started a store here in the 1890s. Satterdahlburg would have been too long a name, so they used his first name — and even shortened that. This road goes north to U.S. Route 60, the primary east-west highway before construction of Interstate 10. About 10 miles east on U.S. 60 is the tiny roadside community of Salome, made famous by Dick Wick Hall, a 1920s humorist-philosopher who lived in the area. Among his many outlandish stories, Hall claimed that he owned a canteen-carrying frog that was seven years old and couldn't swim because, in the bone-dry desert, it had never seen a pool of water.

44 Kofa Mountains — This massive range can be seen on the horizon to the south for the next 20 miles. Unlike many

unusual-sounding Arizona place names, Kofa is not derived from an Indian term. It is an acronym for the early King of Arizona (K of A) mine that operated in the area. On early maps they were called the S.H. Mountains, initials of a synonym for outhouse, which miners in the area felt a portion of the range resembled. The vast Kofa National Wildlife Area is populated by desert bighorn sheep, mule deer, coyotes, bobcats, golden eagles, and many other wildlife forms.

38 **New Water Mountains and Eagle Eye** — South of the highway, in the nearby New Water Mountains, a naturally formed hole penetrates a large rock bench on an upper ridge. Eagle Eye, as it is called, can be seen at a 9 o'clock position. It appears just west of a high pinnacle that protrudes above the ridge. No one is sure of the origin of the name New Water.

34 **Black Mesa** — To the south, at the end of the Plomosa (Spanish for "leaden") Mountains, Black Mesa was the site of early gold, silver, and lead mines.

Exit 31 **General Patton's Training Center** — In 1906, George Bouse, an enterprising developer, established the small community that carries his name 18 miles north on State Route 72. For 37 years nothing much developed, but in 1943 Gen. George Patton arrived with his tanks and thousands of troops to train for the World War II campaign in the deserts of North Africa. For a while, the tiny town was a beehive of activity. But today, Bouse is once again very quiet.

23 Dome Rock Mountains — From this milepost another range of imposing desert mountains rises directly to the west. Much of this range consists of granite and volcanic rocks. To the south, you can see layers of sedimentary rock that have tilted upward, revealing the various layers that were created over millions of years.

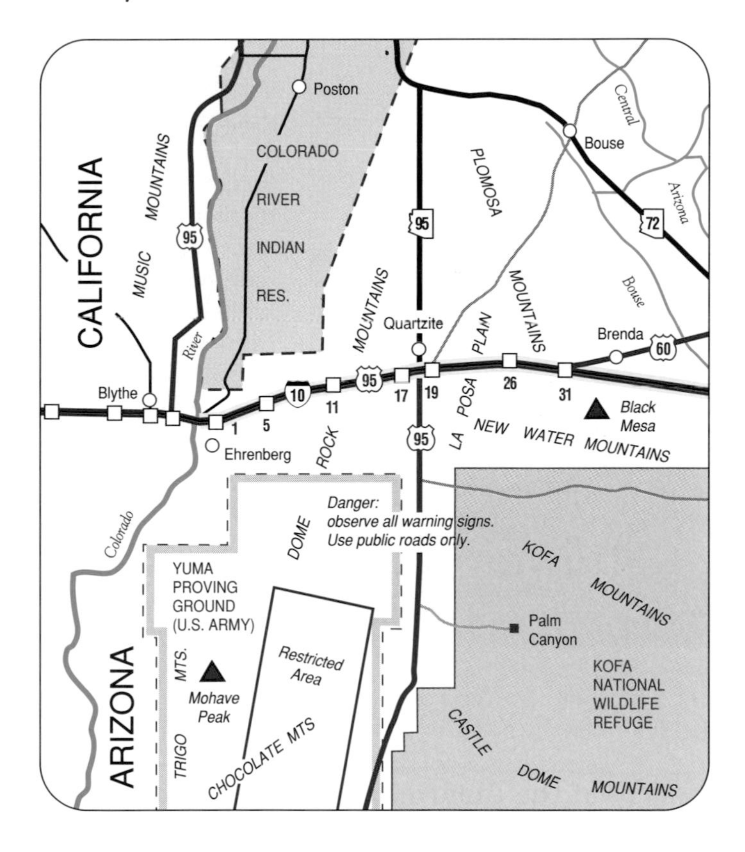

Exit 19 Quartzsite — Established as a fort in 1856 by Charles Tyson, this location was originally called Tyson Wells. When a mining boom took place around 1897 the name was changed to Quartzsite in honor of the metamorphic rock (quartz) that frequently contains gold. In recent decades, people from northern states have discovered the area's sunshine and laid-back lifestyle. Especially in winter months, "snowbirds" flock to Quartzsite in their RVs and trailers. Every February Quartzsite is the site of one of the world's largest gem and mineral shows.

18 Hi Jolly Monument — In 1857, Lt. Edward F. Beale surveyed a wagon road across northern Arizona that later became

the famous Route 66 and then Interstate 40. Beale's survey included the experimental use of camels as military beasts of burden. While the animals were well suited to the arid Southwest – they could travel long distances without water and thrived on natural forage – the camels frightened horses and mules and the muleskinners hated the smell of the beasts. North African camel drivers were brought in, and the best known was Hadji Ali (quickly Americanized to Hi Jolly). The Civil War brought an end to the experiment, and the camels were sold off. Hi Jolly married and settled in Arizona. His monument, a pyramid crowned with a camel, stands in the Quartzsite cemetery one block north of the center of town.

10 **Valley of the Colorado River** — You are now descending into a broad valley cut by the Colorado River. This powerful river, a major force in the formation of the Grand Canyon, begins in the Rocky Mountains of Colorado and flows 1,450 miles to the Gulf of California. Its northernmost tributary, the Green River, has its headwaters in Wyoming.

5 **Rest Area** — Near this milepost is a roadside rest area with ramadas, picnic tables, and rest rooms. From this point, you have an unobstructed view of California.

3 **Gravel Deposits** — In this area you pass through deep layers of sand and gravel laid down by the Colorado River millions of years ago. Across the ensuing millennia, the river has cut its way down to the present stream bed.

1 Ehrenberg — Just south of this milepost is the community of Ehrenberg. In the 1870s it was an important port for the paddle wheel steamboats that brought passengers and supplies upstream from the Gulf of California. "Of all the dreary, miserable-looking settlements that one could possibly imagine, it was the worst. It was an important shipping point for freight to the interior and there always was an army officer stationed there," wrote Martha Summerhayes of the town in the 1870s.

Hermann Ehrenberg, the town's namesake, was a widely traveled German mining engineer who came to Arizona via Louisiana, Texas (where he fought in the war for independence), Oregon, and Hawaii, eventually landing here in 1854.

0 Crossing the Border — At the approximate center of this bridge across the Colorado River, you leave Arizona and enter California.

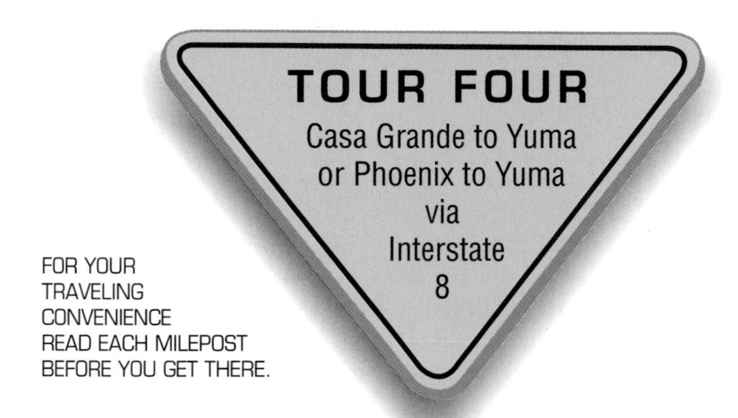

FOR YOUR
TRAVELING
CONVENIENCE
READ EACH MILEPOST
BEFORE YOU GET THERE.

Starting Points — Your tour can begin at the east end of Interstate 8 near Casa Grande and proceed west. Interstate exit numbers and mileposts will appear in descending order. An alternate route starts west of Phoenix on Interstate 10 at Exit 112.

Along the Way — This tour passes through a vast area of the lower Sonoran Desert originally populated by a hardy, prehistoric culture known as the Hohokam. They lived in the region for nearly 1,600 years before disappearing around A.D. 1350.

Much of this area is unpopulated except for small communities along the highway. Portions of this area are rich in agriculture because of irrigation water from dams and deep wells.

More than 6,500 square miles on both sides of the highway are dedicated to restricted military use, two wildlife refuges, and an isolated national monument.

MILEPOST HIGHLIGHTS

Section 1 — Departing from Casa Grande. (To depart from Phoenix, an alternate route, see Section 2, page 52, for corresponding text.)

Casa Grande — Established as a railroad stop in 1879, this community of about 20,000 residents was named for the prehistoric Casa Grande ruins the National Park Service maintains as a national monument about 20 miles northeast of the town's business district. The ancient Hohokam extensively irrigated and farmed the flatlands around Casa Grande

(Left) Four principle plants shown in this lush scene west of Casa Grande include saguaro cactus, palo verde trees, creosote bushes, and burr sage.

long before the arrival of Europeans. Today, this region continues to be a major agricultural area producing primarily cotton and livestock feed. Casa Grande offers a selection of motels, restaurants, and retail services.

171 Santa Cruz River — This historic river starts its course in the San Rafael Valley of southern Arizona, runs south into Mexico, then turns abruptly and flows back into Arizona near Nogales. It continues northward 182 miles to join the Gila River about 40 miles northwest of this crossing. Usually the river displays a dry stream bed, but after fierce desert thunderstorms it can become a raging flood.

Exit 167 Estrella Mountains — Far to the north, at about a 2 o'clock position, the blue outline of the rugged Estrella Mountains rises into the desert sky. Maricopa County protects the northern third of this waterless range as a desert mountain park; most of the rest lies on the Gila River Indian Reservation. The city of Phoenix lies just north of the range's eastern slopes.

Exit 161 Papago Indian Reservation — To the south, stretching across more than 4,000 square miles, lies the homeland of the Tohono O'odham Nation. In 1986 the tribe revised their constitution and petitioned the Secretary of the Interior to change their name. Papago is a Spanish corruption of the word meaning "bean eater." Tohono O'odham means "desert people" in their native language. This is the second largest reservation in the United States, exceeded only by the Navajo reservation that encompasses northeastern Arizona and parts of Utah and New

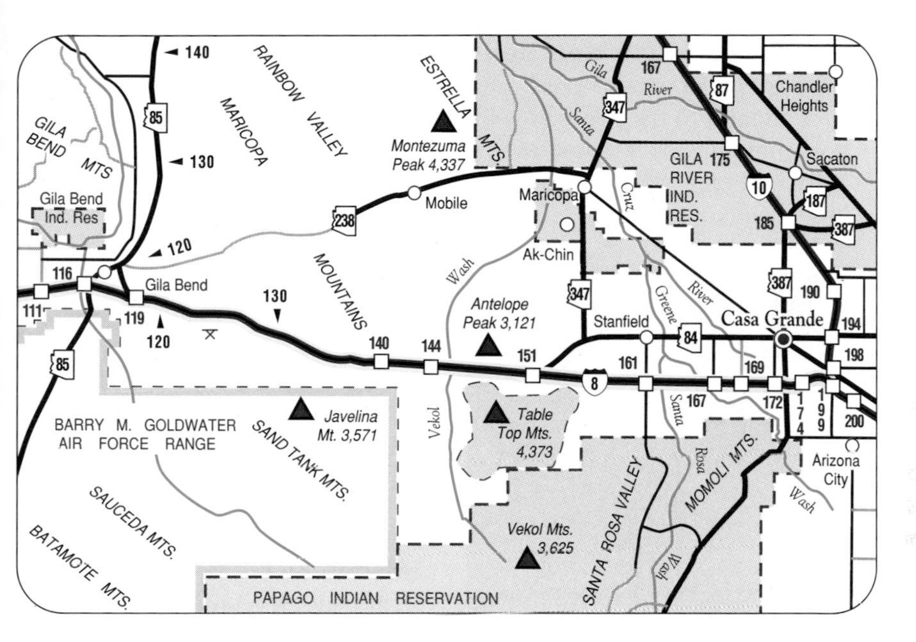

Mexico. The 8,000 member Tohono O'odham tribe is largely uninterested in tourist trade. Services on the reservation are limited and many of the roads are unpaved.

158 Table Top Mountains — Like many flat-topped mountains of the Southwest, the most prominent peak in this range (4,373 feet elevation) is capped by a horizontal lava flow highly resistant to erosion. The lava is quite recent, but the main portion of the range is Precambrian granite, which, in its oldest form, can approach 1.7 billion years.

146 Vekol Wash — The broad valley and the wash that runs through it bear the same name as a silver mine, known to the Pima Indians as the Vekol ("grandmother"). In 1880, the Pimas revealed its location (in the Vekol Mountains 15 miles south of this milepost) to brothers John and Lucian Walker. Mining interests offered the Walkers $150,000 for the property, but they declined it — a sound decision since the Vekol later produced more than a million dollars in silver.

138 Maricopa and Sand Tank Mountains — The Maricopa Mountains north of the highway and the Sand Tank Mountains to the south are similar in composition to the Table Top Mountains. Formed of uplifted Precambrian granite, they have been capped by more recent lava flows that occurred just a few million years ago.

Wesley Holden

135 World's Tallest Saguaro — Saguaros grow in profusion in this part of the state. Able to live beyond 200 years, saguaros often exceed 30 feet in height. The world's tallest saguaro, listed in *The 1987 Guinness Book of Records* at 57 feet, 11 inches, is located in the Maricopa Mountains several miles north of this milepost.

125 Cholla Forest — South of the highway grows a small forest of cholla cactus. Often called jumping cholla, this cactus doesn't really jump, but has nearly transparent spines and loosely jointed branches that break easily when brushed against. The spines attach themselves to almost anything they touch.

124 Roadside Rest Area — Beyond this milepost is a rest stop with ramadas, picnic tables, and rest rooms.

Exit 119 Gila Bend — This exit leads to Gila Bend, so named because the town is located where the south-running Gila River takes a sharp westward turn. Note: To continue your tour along Interstate 8, skip ahead to Section 3, page 55.

Section 2 — Departing from Phoenix. Start your trip by driving west on Interstate 10 to Exit 112, then south on State Route 85. Mileposts will be in descending order to Gila Bend.

Exit 112 — Head south on State Route 85. After a drive of approximately 35 miles, you will turn west, pass through the desert community of Gila Bend and intersect with Interstate 8 for

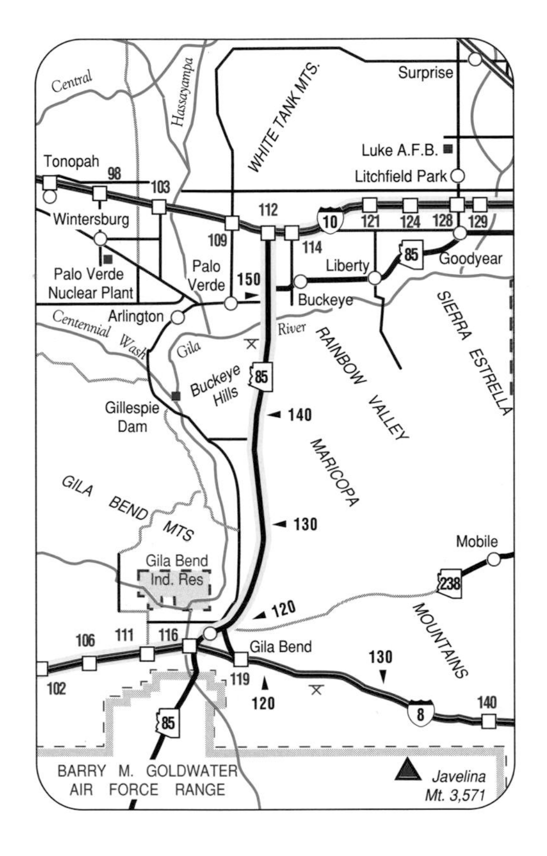

the balance of your journey. Sequencing begins with Milepost 154 and continues in descending order as you turn onto Interstate 8 and drive to the California border.

149 Tamarisk Jungle — Beyond this milepost, the highway passes through an area that is overgrown with extremely dense tamarisk shrubbery. These hardy plants, originally imported from the Mideast, thrive in moist, saline soil and have spread along most of Arizona's desert rivers and streams, choking out many native plants. While almost impossible for humans to penetrate, a tamarisk jungle offers safe haven for desert wildlife.

148 Gila River — Dams along its course have interrupted the flow of the Gila River, but in earlier years it was considered one of America's great rivers. Starting east of the New Mexico border at an altitude of 9,993 feet, the Gila flows across the entire width of Arizona to join the Colorado River at the California border. Much of the Gila's impounded water is used for agricultural irrigation.

147 Greenbelt Overlook — Beyond this milepost, a paved road to the west winds through desert foothills to an overlook that provides a panoramic view of a large section of countryside, including the meandering greenbelt created by the Gila River.

146 Roadside Stop — Just past this milepost is a rest area with ramadas and picnic tables, but no rest rooms.

144 Buckeye Hills Recreation Area — A dirt road leads west into the nearby Buckeye Hills where picnic and camping areas provide solitude and desert scenery, but no water. On the far side of this rugged little desert range is Gillespie Dam, diverting the waters of the Gila River to irrigate a major agricultural area that you will see during your southward journey.

142 Gillespie Dam — The dam was built by the Gila Water Company in 1921 and named for its chief engineer, Frank A. Gillespie.

A bandit was once killed near here. A 40-pound shipment of gold bullion was being taken to Phoenix from the Vulture Mine at Wickenburg. About half way, the mine superintendent, driver, and mounted guard were waylaid and killed by three bandits. A posse was quickly formed and followed the bandits' trail south, catching up with them at Gillespie Dam. In the gunfight that followed, the gold was recovered, one bandit was killed, and the other two fled towards Mexico, never to be heard from again.

138 Gila Bend and Maricopa Mountains — To the west rise the Gila Bend Mountains. The tallest point, Woolsey Peak (3,170 feet), was named for King S. Woolsey who arrived in Arizona territory in 1860 almost penniless. He later earned a fortune in mining, ranching, and flour milling. The world's tallest saguaro cactus grows in the rugged Maricopa Mountains to the east of the highway. Listed in *The 1987 Guinness Book of Records*, it has been measured at 57 feet, 11 inches.

124 Historic Marker, Mormon Battalion — In October of 1846, a volunteer U.S. Army unit made up entirely of Mormons embarked from Santa Fe, New Mexico Territory, under the command of Capt. Philip St. George Cooke. Part of Gen. Stephen Kearny's Army of the West, the unit was to locate and build a southern route to California. The Mormon Battalion passed through this area shortly after Christmas, 1846. The marker near this milepost is one of many across the Southwest that commemorate the path of the Mormon Battalion.

Many gold-seeking forty-niners used this route along the Gila on their way to California, as did the Butterfield Overland Stage from 1858-61. It was commonly called the Gila Trail or the Butterfield Trail.

Section 3 — Continuing from Gila Bend to Yuma.

Gila Bend — The town was so named because the Gila River, which heads in a southerly direction for some 30 miles, takes a sudden westward turn just north of town. Gila Bend (pop. 2,000) has served travelers through most of its existence. It began as a ranch, then became a stage stop on the Butterfield Overland Stage, a railway station and watering stop for steam powered trains, and a stop on the route of the first U.S. highway between Phoenix and San Diego. Today this roadside community, which also serves a large agricultural and ranching district, offers motels, restaurants, and retail services. The Gila Bend Tourist Information Center and Historical Museum is located on the main business loop through town.

114 Barry M. Goldwater Air Force Range — Directly south of Interstate 8 is the vast Air Force firing range named for former U.S. Sen. Barry Goldwater. The range starts about 25 miles east of Gila Bend and continues west for nearly 130 miles. Varying from 15 to 30 miles in width, this area of approximately 2,500 square miles is the largest gunnery range in the western world. It is uninhabited and strictly off-limits. The only road across the area is State Route 85, which leads to the mining community of Ajo, then beyond to Organ Pipe Cactus National Monument and the Mexican border.

112 Paloma Ranch Agricultural District — Stretching for many miles to the north and west is the acreage of the Paloma Ranch ("dove" in Spanish). The ranch took its name from an 1890s settlement called Palomas, which was established on the north bank of the Gila River 30 miles farther west. The community was so named because of the white wing doves that migrated there each summer. Today, this 85,000-acre spread, irrigated with water from deep wells, is the largest irrigated farm in the world. Cotton and cattle feed are the principal crops.

Exit 102 Painted Rock Park — Approximately 15 miles north on Painted Rock Road is a boulder-strewn area that is covered with hundreds of ancient Indian petroglyphs (figures of people and animals) that date back to the Hohokam people of about A.D. 1400. Nearby are camping sites, ramadas, picnic tables, grills, and rest rooms. Defacing or removing petroglyphs and artifacts is illegal and carries stiff penalties.

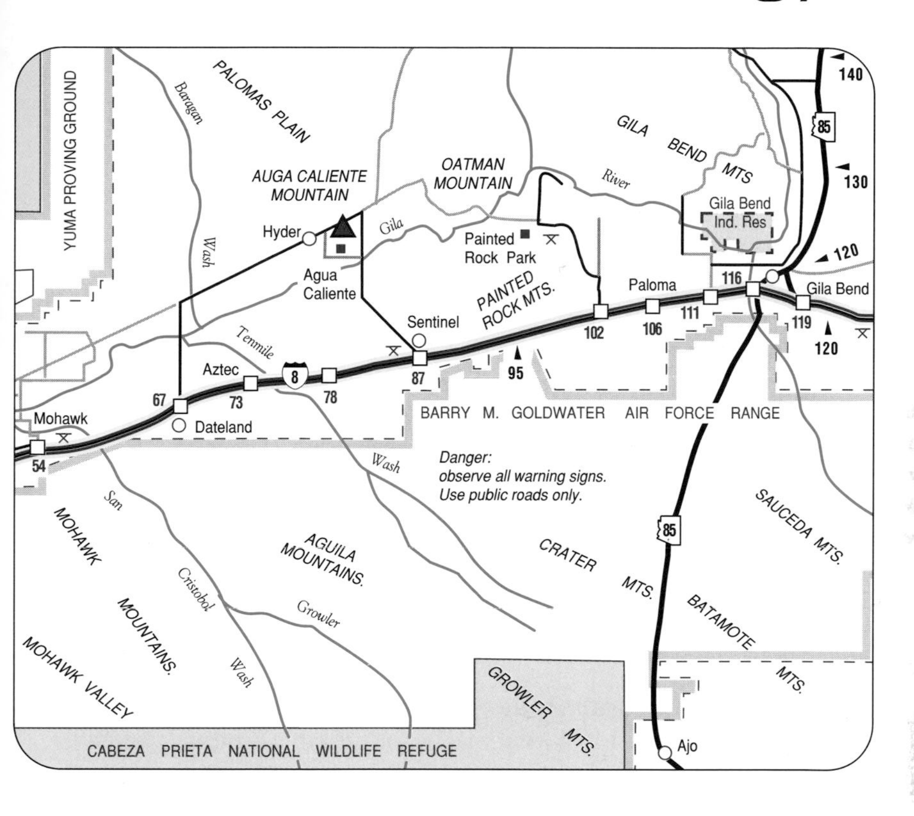

95 Oatman Massacre Site — About 12 miles north of the highway, at a 3 o'clock position, is Oatman Mountain. On the flats just south of the mountain, the Oatman family, traveling by wagon to California in 1851, was set upon by a group of renegade Indians. Royce Oatman, his wife, and four of their seven children were killed. A son, Lorenzo, was thrown off the mesa and left for dead, but he survived. Daughters Mary Ann, 8, and Olive, 12, were taken captive. The renegades traded the girls to the peaceful Mohave Indians. Unfortunately, Mary Ann, who was sickly, died a year later. After his recovery from near death, Lorenzo pursued rumors of a white girl living with an Indian family for five years. He found Olive and traded a horse, some blankets, and beads to get her back.

93 Sentinel Volcanic Field — You are now entering the Sentinel volcanic field where chunks of lava are scattered across the landscape for the next 20 miles. The eruptions of lava in this area were extremely fluid and spread easily from vents in the earth. Consequently, there are none of the volcanic peaks and cinder cones usually associated with volcanic action.

Exit 87 Road to Agua Caliente — Agua Caliente (Spanish for "hot water"), about 9 miles north at this exit, had a hot spring the early Indians used for therapeutic purposes. By 1873, the location had become a popular health resort that attracted white clientele from near and far. Seeking to increase business, the owners attempted to enlarge the bathing area with dynamite. Instead the blast caused the spring to dry up. Agua Caliente became a ghost town.

Hyder, 3 miles north of Agua Caliente, was also one of the sites of Gen. George S. Patton's World War II desert training centers. Very little remains of the old camp, but veterans sometimes return to visit the site.

85 Sentinel Rest Area — In the lava field beyond this milepost is a rest stop with ramadas, picnic tables, and rest rooms.

Exit 78 Aguila Mountains — A formation in these rugged mountains to the south (9 o'clock position) is said to resemble the eye and beak of an eagle. Aguila is Spanish for "eagle."

South of these mountains, and beyond the Barry M. Goldwater Air Force Range, is the Cabeza Prieta National Wildlife Refuge (1,400 square miles). Bordering the refuge on the east is Organ Pipe Cactus National Monument (500 square miles). Except for State Route 85, which goes through the monument, the only road (actually a dirt track) requires a four-wheel-drive vehicle and wilderness equipment. Off-road travel requires permission in advance from the Cabeza Prieta National Wildlife Refuge in Ajo.

79 Independence Rock — Along the Gila River, about 10 miles to the north, dozens of Kit Carson's trailblazers scratched their names on a cliff of a mesa locally known as Independence Rock.

68-69 Dateland — Three Army Air Corps auxiliary training fields were built near here during World War II. Each facility is comprised of three 5,000-foot-long runways forming a giant triangle. All that remains today is their cracked concrete and a few slabs where buildings once stood. Watch closely on the north side of the freeway for evidence of one of the fields.

Exit 67 Mohawk Mountains — Some say these wildly tossed mountains to the southwest (11 o'clock) were named for their resemblance to the straight-standing hairstyle of a Mohawk warrior. Composed of nearly vertical rock slopes and with no water, desert mountains like these are home to a wide variety of hardy birds and animals that are equipped to cope with the harsh conditions.

63 Sleeping Giant — In the small mountain range to the north look for the head of the sleeping giant. His nose is the highest point and his open mouth is to the left. You won't hear him snore because, as you get nearer, he will close his mouth.

57 Mohawk Rest Area — The rest stop beyond this milepost offers ramadas, picnic tables, and rest rooms.

50 Agricultural — North of the highway a rich strip of irrigated agricultural land extends for the next 50 miles to the California border. Beyond this farmland is the U.S. Army's Yuma Proving Ground. This restricted area is set aside for artillery testing. Still farther north lies the Kofa National Wildlife Refuge.

Exit 42 Tacna — Originally a stage station called Antelope Hill, the settlement became a stop on the railroad, and was renamed Tacna.

This incarnation expired and in the early 1920s Max B. Noah arrived there with a barrel of gasoline and a hand pump and set up shop. He found the old railroad sign and, perhaps to save a dime, called his place Tacna. He was a colorful character, spinner of tall tales, and a good businessman, eventually developing a town complete with his restaurant, Noah's Ark. He sold it all at public auction in the 1940s.

Noah wrote this tall tale about the name: "In the 17th century, a Greek padre named Tachnapolis found his way into Arizona from California and spent his last days with the Indians around here. They naturally shortened his name to Tachna or Tacha. As he grew older, he always had a fire in his hut and a light at night. The Papagos called his place Tachna — 'the bright spot' or 'bright light' — and the word has come to mean that in their language."

29 Gila Mountains and the Devil's Highway — Directly ahead rise the Gila Mountains, which run a southeasterly course and join the Tinajas Altas ("high tanks" in Spanish) Mountains farther to the south. Essentially waterless and impassable, these mountain ranges provided a formidable barrier

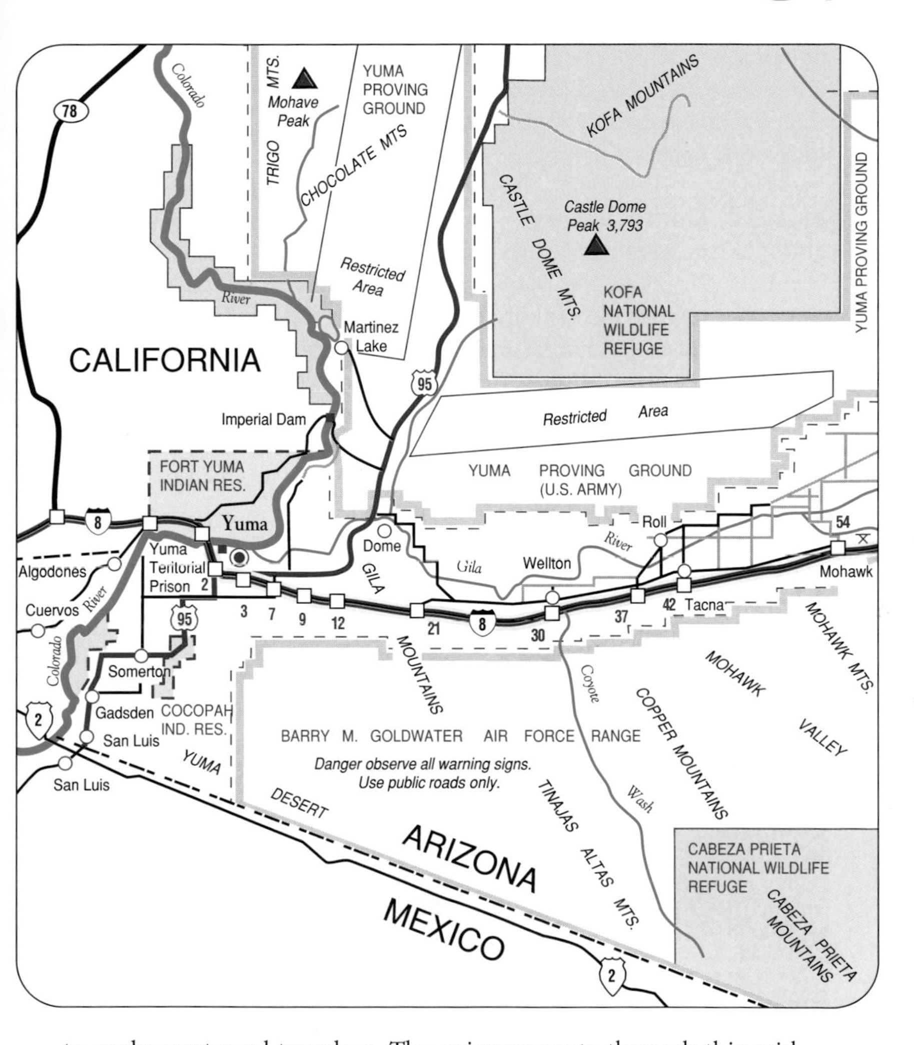

to early westward travelers. The primary route through this arid region was known as El Camino del Diablo. "The Devil's Highway" was used first in 1697 by Father Eusebio Kino. It ran westerly across northern Mexico, crossed into what is now Arizona near Organ Pipe Cactus National Monument, snaked through the desert to the mountain barrier, then turned north to the Gila River. Travelers endured more than 150 miles of parched desert before reaching water. The route was aptly named — it was a tortuous path of heat, thirst, and, for many, death.

25 Muggins Mountains and Ligurta Wash — A frontier-days prospector, whose name is no longer recalled, named the range of mountains directly north of the highway for his beloved burro, Muggins. Ligurta Wash, just ahead, was named by someone who noticed the profusion of lizards in the immediate area, but didn't have a great command of Spanish. "Ligurta" is apparently an anglicized version of the Spanish word for lizard, *lagarto.*

Exit 21 Dome Valley — A few miles north of the highway gold placers were discovered in 1858 and a town named Gila City boomed. Miners by the thousands flocked to the area causing a town of a few adobe buildings and hundreds of tents to spring up. In describing the rapid influx of merchants and gamblers, J. Ross Brown wrote, "There was everything in Gila City within a few months but a church and a jail." In less than 10 years the gold disappeared and so did Gila City. When the railroad came through, the siding there was named Dome for the locally famous Castle Dome Mountains. It subsequently became a major ore shipping point for southwestern Arizona. Today it is a major agricultural area.

18 Valley of the Colorado River — Ahead is a lowland carved by the force of the Colorado River, which in this area flows at an elevation of about 110 feet above sea level. This mighty river enters north-central Arizona from Utah and is responsible for cutting the mile-deep Grand Canyon. Numerous dams along the course of the Colorado have tamed the wild river and slowed its flow. In the 1800s the river was navigable. For decades steamboats and other water craft used it as an avenue of transportation and commerce.

15 Snowbirds and RV Parks — If you pass this point during the summer months, you'll see signs that advertise mostly empty RV parks. However, in the winter, nearly 50,000 "snowbirds" (people fleeing the cold weather in the northern states) cover this area of the desert with their recreational vehicles, campers, and house trailers.

Exit 7 Harsh Desert, Lush Farmland — The view to the north provides proof that desert soil needs only water to be transformed. Just off the highway, parched land sustains only hardy creosote bushes. But a short distance away, the irrigated fields glow emerald green during the growing season. Lettuce is a primary crop in this area.

1 Yuma and Territorial Prison State Park — A pleasant community of about 50,000 residents, Yuma offers a good selection of motels, restaurants, and retail services. The city is also known for its proximity to boating and fishing along the Colorado River. From November through February, the Imperial National Wildlife Refuge just north of town is a magnet for bird watchers.

The old territorial prison, one of Yuma's main attractions, can be reached from this exit. From 1875 until 1909, this infamous prison existed as a veritable Devil's Island on the American desert. In temperatures often exceeding 120 degrees, prisoners were sometimes chained to the rock floors or cast into dark dungeons. Nevertheless, some critics complained that the facility was a "country club" because it had a library, classrooms and an infirmary. Visitors may view the ruins of the prison for a modest admission fee.

0 Colorado River Bridge and California Border 

FOR YOUR TRAVELING CONVENIENCE READ EACH MILEPOST BEFORE YOU GET THERE.

Starting Point — Your journey starts in Tucson, aptly referred to as the Old Pueblo. For a brief profile of this intriguing city turn to page 77. Interstate exit numbers and mileposts will be in ascending order.

Along the Way — This 134-mile trip starts in the Sonoran Desert country that surrounds Tucson, then takes you through undulating hills and grasslands to the New Mexico border. Along the way, rugged mountain ranges, most of them rich in frontier lore, rise against a limitless sky. You can stop to visit a museum that displays old military aircraft and flight memorabilia. Another museum is dedicated to Indians of the Southwest. Yet another traces the life of a famous cowboy singer and movie star.

Side roads can take you to Tombstone, "the town too tough to die"; to the mountain stronghold of the famous Apache chieftain Cochise; and to the crumbling remains of historic Fort Bowie. You will cross a river that runs north, and pass an ancient lake bed that today is only miles and miles of blowing sand. This portion of Interstate 10 roughly follows the route of the old Butterfield Stage (1858-1861).

MILEPOST HIGHLIGHTS

EXIT 263

Overpass View — From this exit vantage point in southeast Tucson, you have a good view of several impressive mountain ranges: directly to the north, the Santa Catalina Mountains, highest point 9,157 feet; to the northeast, the Rincon Mountains, elevation 8,666 feet; and due south, the Santa Rita Mountains, highest peak 9,453 feet. Tucson gets 7.5 inches of moisture per year while the top of the

(Left) Willcox Playa, near Milepost 330, is a favorite stopping place for sandhill cranes every autumn.

Catalinas receives more than 40 inches. With their upper ridges covered in pine trees, these and other mountains in southeastern Arizona deserve the nickname "sky islands."

Exit 267 Pima Air Museum — Two miles north on Valencia Road you'll find one of the nation's most impressive collections of old U.S. military aircraft. The museum displays more than 160 well-preserved relics, many from World War II. Other exhibits include memorabilia representing early eras of flight. Admission fees are modest for adults; children under 10 get in free. Open daily, 9 A.M. to 5 P.M.

Exit 273 Slopes of the Rincon Mountains — To the northeast, notice the steep slopes of the Rincons and the huge areas of exposed rock. Like many of the high mountain ranges of southern Arizona, the Rincons are made up of great domes of granite and other metamorphic rock forms created by the cooling of molten magma approximately 1.5 billion years ago.

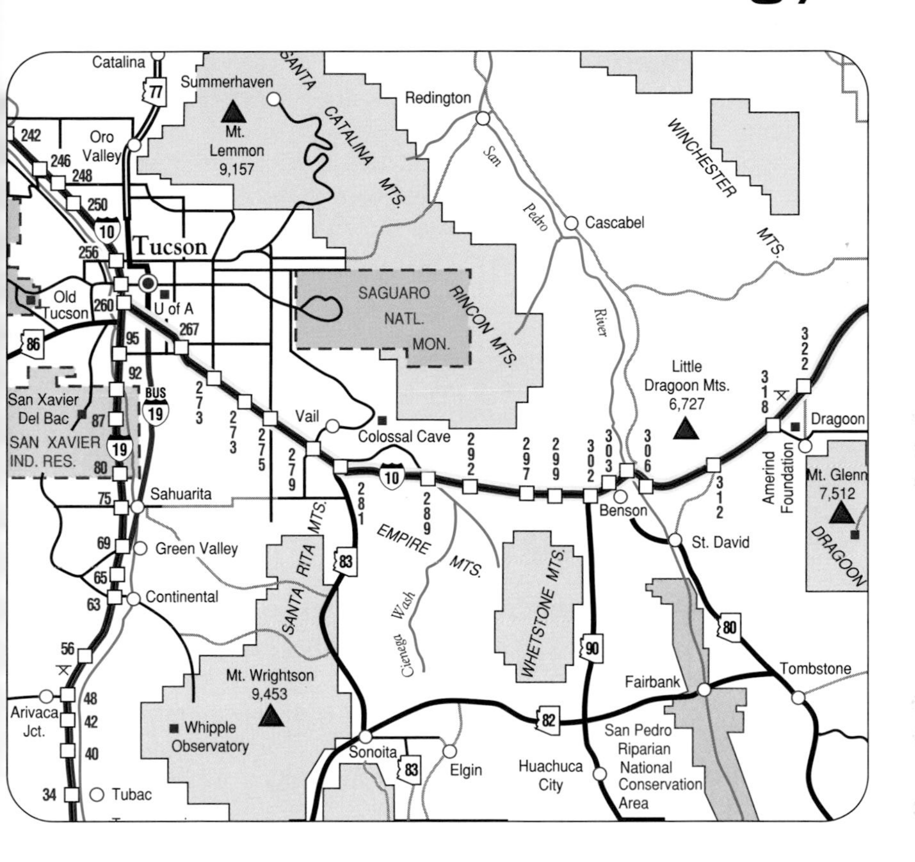

Exit 275 Saguaro National Monument — Travel 9 miles north on Houghton Road and the Old Spanish Trail to find the eastern portion of Saguaro National Monument. In 1933, these 3,520 cactus-studded acres of high desert on the western slope of the Rincon Mountains were set aside as a national monument. In this setting, saguaros grow in profusion, sometimes living beyond 200 years and attaining heights of more than 40 feet. The monument and visitors center are open daily. A modest fee is charged per vehicle.

Exit 279 Colossal Cave — At this exit, Vail Road goes north 7 miles to a network of limestone caverns where legends say outlaw gold still lies hidden. Supposedly, the outlaws were using the cave for their hideout. A posse tracked them here, but while its members waited outside, the outlaws buried the loot and escaped via another opening. Dripping water containing mineral elements has decorated the underground rooms with bizarre formations of hanging stalactites and upstanding stalagmites. Open daily. There is an admission fee.

Exit 281 Route to Cattle Country — State Route 83 winds south through some of Arizona's finest livestock-raising country to the old cattle and mining towns of Sonoita and Patagonia. Flanked by the Santa Rita Mountains to the west and the Whetstones to the east, this route conveys a sense of the West as it once was. Here you also make the transition from the lower Sonoran Desert of saguaro and other cactus to grasslands studded with yucca and ocotillo.

284 Davidson Canyon — During the era of Apache warfare, the eroded canyon just east of this milepost was a dangerous place. Apaches killed a large number of travelers, prospectors, and wagon drivers in this area. In 1872, a Lieutenant Stewart and a Corporal Black were ambushed at Davidson Canyon. When discovered by searchers, the bodies exhibited more than 100 arrow, lance, and knife wounds.

289 Cienega Wash — *Cienega* is Spanish for marsh or swamp. North of the interstate, and not far from this desert wash, a stage station was built in 1858 to provide water for the horses. The railroad erected Pantano Station nearby in 1880 to take advantage of the water for its steam engines. The history of this area consists almost entirely of Apache raids, stage robberies, and train holdups. Very tough country.

296 Whetstone Mountains — The imposing range of mountains directly to the south were once called Mesteños ("wild horse") Mountains because herds of wild mustangs lived in the canyons. The name evolved to Whetstone Mountains after a large deposit of novaculite, a mineral used in the making of whetstones, was discovered.

Exit 302 State Route 90 — This highway leads south 35 miles to Sierra Vista (pop. 35,000) and Fort Huachuca. The U.S. Army first established the fort in 1877 as a frontier outpost. In more recent decades it has served as the Army's Information Systems Command, Intelligence Center and School, and Electronic Proving Ground. The base has an excellent military museum. On special occasions there are public performances by B Troop, a volunteer unit that commemorates the famous 4th Cavalry Troop of the Apache wars.

Exit 303 Benson — On a slope that descends to the valley of the San Pedro River, this exit leads to the town of Benson. Since the coming of the railroad in 1880, Benson has served the surrounding mining, agricultural, and ranching areas. From here, U.S. Route 80 goes south to the legendary town of Tombstone, site of Wyatt Earp's shoot-out at the OK Corral, then on to the once-major mining and smelting communities of Bisbee and Douglas.

Exit 306 **San Pedro River** — This river, which is usually dry, starts in Sonora, Mexico, and winds its way north through Arizona for more than 100 miles until it joins the Gila River near the mining community of Winkelman. This valley has been a major pathway for thousands of years. The San Pedro has witnessed the migration of early man since the days of the mammoths (several kill sites have been excavated near here), attempts at settlement by early Spanish explorers, the violent clash of Apache and white cultures, the route of the Butterfield Overland Stage, and the first railroad across the southern U.S.

307 **Battle of the Bulls** — In the area just south of this milepost, the 1846 road-building military unit known as the Mormon Battalion was attacked by a herd of ferocious wild bulls. Well armed, the soldiers eventually dispatched the animals, but not before a number of men, horses, and mules were gored.

316 **Entering Texas Canyon** — For the next 4 miles, on your way to a mountain pass, you will climb through a wonderland of oddly sculptured quartz monzonite porphyry rock formations that closely resemble granite with warts (actually

protruding crystals of feldspar). These rock formations were originally giant blocks that were cracked in countless places by weathering and the wrenching movements of the earth. They then eroded into the individual boulders you see today. David Adams, an early settler from Texas, named the canyon for his native state.

Exit 318 The Amerind Foundation Museum — This is a highly recommended side trip to a secluded enclave of art and culture. Almost hidden in a boulder-strewn canyon 1 mile south on the Dragoon Road, the Amerind Foundation offers one of the finest collections of prehistoric Native American artifacts in the Southwest. Also, the foundation's art gallery exhibits an intriguing collection of the works of well-known frontier artists. There is an admission fee.

320 Texas Canyon Rest Area — This pleasant rest area, featuring vending machines, picnic tables, a public phone, and rest rooms, looks south into the Dragoon Mountains where the legendary Apache chieftain Cochise is buried in an unmarked grave. An historic marker provides details of a peace treaty signed by Cochise and the U.S. government in 1872.

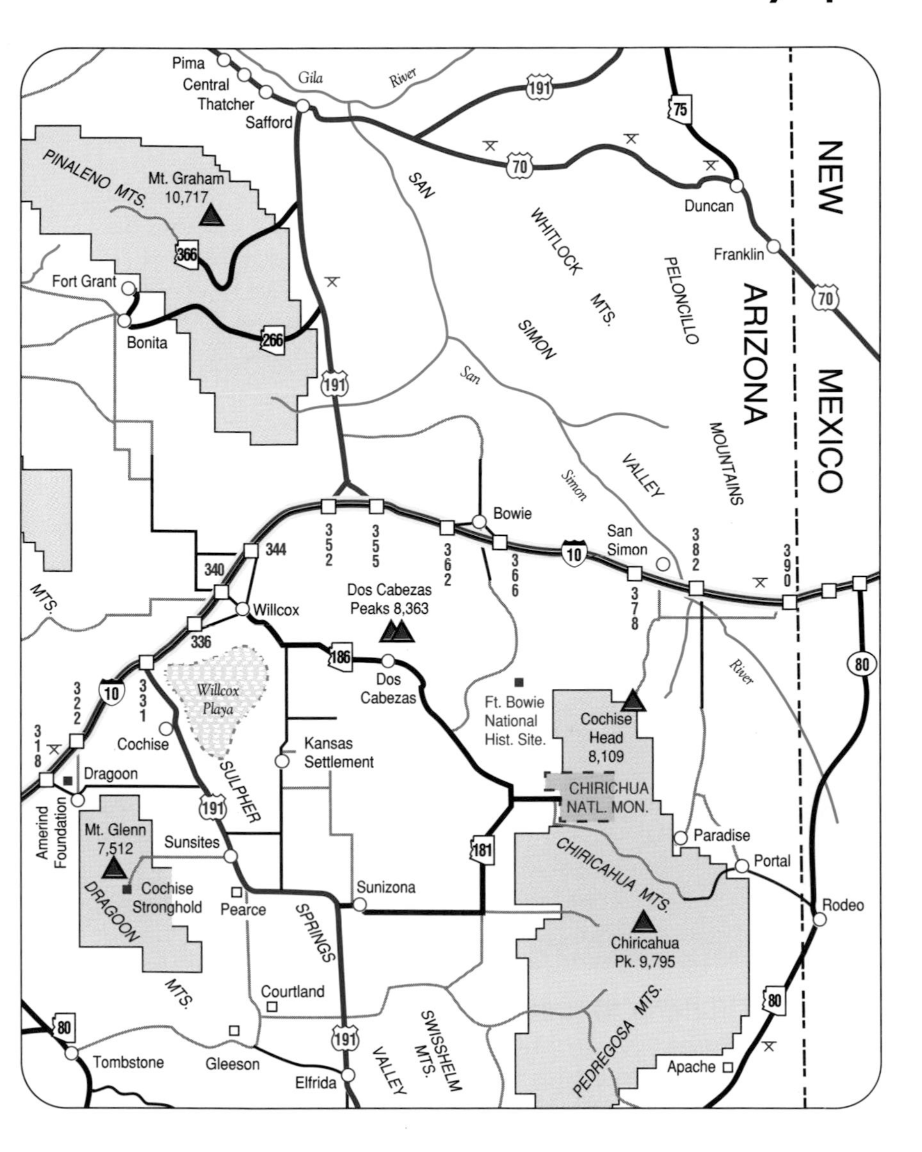

330 Willcox Playa — The giant swath of land in the valley to the east and south was once a prehistoric lake. Today, Willcox Playa is known for its blowing sand and deceptive mirages. During World War II, a U.S. Navy pilot tried landing his disabled seaplane in the extremely shallow lake. It remained stuck in the mud for some time before it could be hauled away. Rain and runoff from the surrounding mountains occasionally accumulate to form a lake perhaps a foot deep. The playa and the surrounding irrigated agricultural area attract a variety of bird life, including the sandhill crane. The tall peaks directly to the east are the Dos Cabezas (Spanish for "two heads") Mountains. The protrusions on the highest peak, at 8,363 feet, are the *cabezas.* To the south of the range is a town by the same name.

Exit 331 **Dragoon Mountains** — Due south, in the rugged wilderness of the Dragoon Mountains, Cochise and his warriors hid out during the years before the peace treaty of 1872. The area is still called Cochise Stronghold. A drive of about 30 miles leads to a campground area in the shadow of 7,512-foot Mt. Glenn. A small camping fee is charged.

334 **Pinaleno Mountains** — To the north, the often snow-capped Pinaleno (a Spanish derivation of "pinal," the Apache word for deer) Mountains rise abruptly from the desert floor to 10,717 feet at the highest peak, Mt. Graham. Another sky island, Mt. Graham is the greatest elevation rise in the state and encompasses all the climatic zones encountered from southern Arizona to northern Canada. During the Apache campaigns, Fort Grant was located near the base of the Pinaleno's southwestern slope. It became a bustling Army post visited by nearly everyone who passed through Arizona, including Billy the Kid. High atop Heliograph Peak (10,028 feet) the Army located a mirrored, sun-reflecting signaling device to communicate with troops in central and southern Arizona, New Mexico, and all the way to Texas. The heliograph played a significant role in the capture of Geronimo and his band of renegades.

Exit 336 Willcox — Rex Allen grew up in the small town of Willcox and was the only singing cowboy movie star who was actually a cowboy. As a youth, he was afflicted with crossed eyes. His family couldn't afford the necessary operation, but the town responded with contributions. Ever grateful, Allen always maintained close ties with his home town. There is a museum in his honor. Open daily; modest admission fee.

Exit 340 Chiricahua National Monument — The ancestral domain of the Chiricahua Apaches (the people of Cochise and Geronimo) offers deep, forested canyons with some of the most amazing rock formations in the world. This national monument in the Chiricahua Mountains (30 miles southeast) offers a visitors center, hiking, camping, and scenic drives. Modest entry and camping fees are charged.

347 Yucca Plants — You will notice a particularly large stand of yucca plants, identified by their clusters of low-growing, sharply pointed leaves. These plants sprout a tall stalk that blooms from March to June, depending on the plant's location. After flowering, the stalk dries and remains for months. The yucca and the pronuba moth have a symbiotic relationship. The moth fertilizes the yucca and lays its eggs in the flowers. When the young moths hatch, the yucca provides them with nourishment. Neither plant nor insect could survive without the other. Yucca was used by early Indians for making baskets, rope, and sandals. They also ate the fruits and used the roots for making soap.

Exit 352 Gateway to the White Mountains — U.S. Route 191 leads north to the towns of Safford, Clifton, and Morenci and on to Arizona's White Mountains and thickly forested high country. This route, called the Coronado Trail, roughly follows the path Coronado traveled in 1540 while in search of the Seven Cities of Gold. Coronado eventually explored as far north and east as present-day Kansas.

Exit 362 Old Fort Bowie — A turnoff here takes you into the small community of Bowie, established as a station on the railroad. A visit to Fort Bowie Historical Site, 13 miles to the south, requires a 1.5 mile hike to the ruins. Fort Bowie was built in 1862 to protect a spring, the only good surface water for miles. Several bloody battles were fought over the water source during the days of the Butterfield Stage. Fort Bowie became station No. 1 of the heliograph system and headquarters for Gen. Nelson A. Miles' campaign against the Apache.

364 Pistachio Orchards — Pistachio farming in Cochise County is expanding. Currently more than 2,000 acres of pistachio trees produce more than a million pounds of the nuts annually.

Exit 378 San Simon — Established as a railroad stop, the community of San Simon once owned and operated a municipal bath house. An artesian well provided the water; keys to the house were distributed to all citizens.

381 Cochise Head — Look south to the Chiricahua Mountains. On one of the highest ridges, note the profile with rounded forehead and aquiline Indian nose, lips, and chin. This geologic phenomenon, at an elevation of 8,109 feet, is called Cochise Head.

Wesley Holden

Exit 382 Portal and Paradise — South 25 miles as the crow flies, the villages of Portal and Paradise nestle into the eastern slopes of the Chiricahua Mountains. These mountains provide some of the West's finest bird habitats. Portal is the location of the Southwestern Research Station of the American Museum of Natural History. Paradise, in its wooded setting, was once a rip-roaring mining town filled with outlaws, such as the Clanton gang and Curly Bill Brocious. Miners there had to travel to San Simon for supplies. After returning across the long waterless valley, they would take a drink of spring water, relax under the trees, and agree the place was paradise.

385 Peloncillo Mountains — Spanish for "bald," the strangely shaped Peloncillos just to the north were formed by volcanic lava flows and massive deposits of volcanic ash that compacted and fused to give the mountains their peculiar contours. This low-lying range is part of a volcanic region that extends 140 miles from Springerville in the White Mountains to the Mexican border 85 miles south of here.

389 Rest Area — This is your last chance to pause for a leisurely look back at the scenery of southeastern Arizona. Ramadas, picnic tables, and rest rooms are provided before you cross the New Mexico border less than 2 miles to the east.

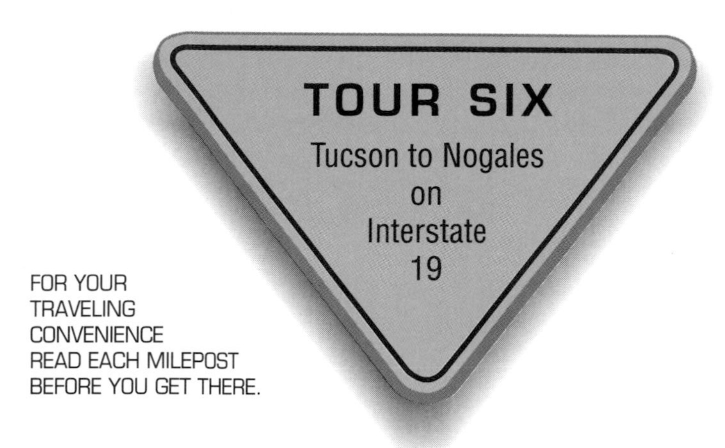

FOR YOUR TRAVELING CONVENIENCE READ EACH MILEPOST BEFORE YOU GET THERE.

Starting Point — Your journey starts in Tucson. This dynamic city, with a metropolitan population of more than 700,000, existed as a community as far back as the first century A.D. when Hohokam Indians tilled the desert soil.

The Spanish incursion began in the 16th century. The area became Mexican property in 1821 and finally became part of the United States with the Gadsden Purchase of 1853. Tucson reflects numerous cultures. Its architecture, street names, restaurants, shops, art, and people are an appealing mix of Indian, Spanish, and Anglo influences.

Tucson highlights include the city's downtown walking tour, the University of Arizona campus, the Arizona-Sonora Desert Museum, and the sprawling movie sets of Old Tucson Studios. With 9,157-foot Mount Lemmon hovering above the desert city, Tucson is a place where winter resort visitors can swim and snow ski on the same day.

Along the Way — From Tucson, Interstate 19 takes you almost due south along the valley of the Santa Cruz River. The route has been used as an avenue of transportation for centuries. In addition to the raw beauty of the land itself, you can visit a nuclear missile silo museum; shop the fine arts and crafts galleries at Tubac; tour the historic mission of Tumacacori; and end your journey with a visit to Old Mexico.

Side trips along the way may include the scenery of a wooded canyon in the towering Santa Rita Mountains, a visit to an astronomical observatory, or a picnic at the edge of a charming little lake.

(Left) Mission San Xavier del Bac, near Exit 92, is considered the finest remaining example of mission architecture in the United States.

MILEPOST HIGHLIGHTS

Note: As a courtesy to visitors going to or from Mexico, this route is marked in kilometers (.62 of a mile). As you proceed south, the markers and exits will be in descending order, going from Exit 99 at Tucson to Exit 4 at Nogales near the international border, a distance of 99 kilometers (63 miles).

Gateway to Desert Fun — Shortly after reaching Interstate 19 from Interstate 10 in South Tucson, you will approach Exit 99 where Ajo Way leads to the Tucson Mountains (about 10 miles west) and a trio of impressive area attractions. The world-renowned Arizona-Sonora Desert Museum features native animal and plant life in natural exhibits and surroundings. Old Tucson Studios evolved from a group of historic movie sets and is now a major amusement area with tours, gunfights, stagecoach rides, and a long list of sightseeing and entertainment attractions. Saguaro National Monument West provides an unusually dense stand of stately saguaro cactus in a rugged mountain setting.

Exit 95B Yaqui Village — Located about 5 miles to the west is the Pasqua Yaqui Indian Village. With their ancestral roots in Mexico, many Yaqui combine their traditional beliefs with the Catholic faith. The Yaqui fled to the U.S. to escape 19th-century Mexican oppression. The village is a reflection of the lifestyle and culture of this small Native American group.

94 View of San Xavier Mission — After passing this kilometer marker you can obtain a good view of San Xavier del Bac, which sits in a flatland area to the west of the interstate. Also known as the "White Dove of the Desert," the mission, which was established by the Jesuit priest Eusebio Francisco Kino in 1700, combines Byzantine and Moorish architectural elements. The exit to the mission is 2 kilometers ahead. Tourists from around the world come to this historic mission where mass is offered every day of the year. You are welcome to visit the grounds and enter the church. There are gift shops, Indian shade-arbor food stands, and a hill that features a small replica of the Grotto of Lourdes.

93 San Xavier Indian Reservation — Just south of this marker, you enter one of the reservation areas set aside for the Tohono O'odham (Papago) Indians. Ancestors of these Native Americans helped construct San Xavier Mission.

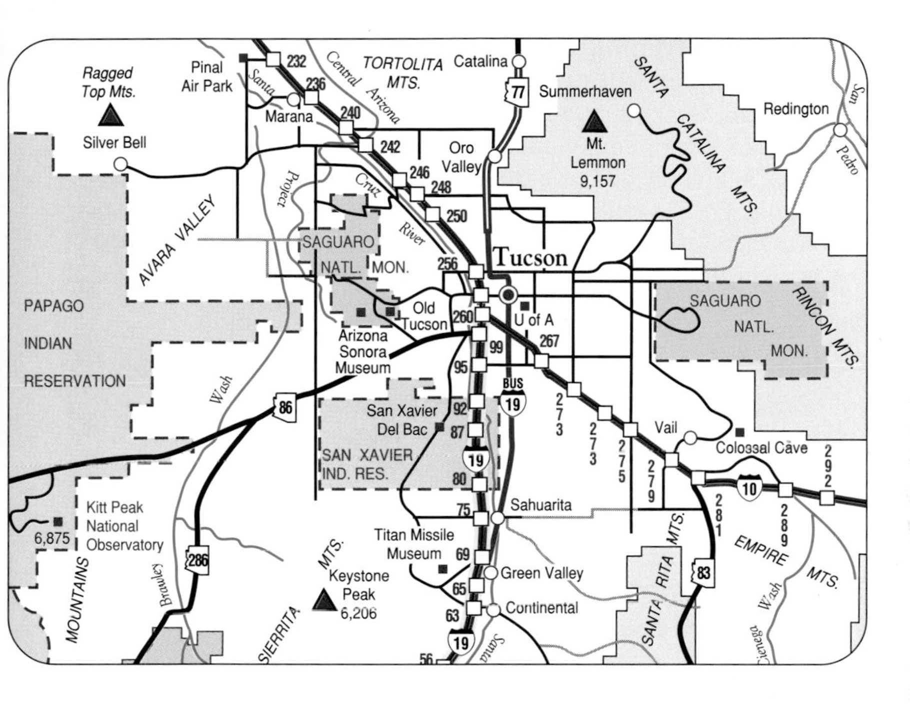

Exit 92 Santa Cruz River — Just south of this exit you will cross the Santa Cruz River, which is dry most of the year. Both the early route of the Santa Cruz Wagon Trail and the modern highway you are driving were constructed to follow the course of this north-running river.

91 Baboquivari Mountains — To the west, at a 2 o'clock position, rise the Baboquivari Mountains. The northernmost peak is the site of Kitt Peak National Optical Observatory, the largest grouping of optical astronomical telescopes in the world. Among its array is the McMath Solar Telescope, the largest of its type in the world.

While the scientific community explores the far reaches of our universe from Kitt Peak, Baboquivari Peak, some 15 miles south, represents the center of the Tohono O'odham Indians' universe. According to their religion, *I'itoy,* the Elder Brother and supreme being, lives in a cave on the west side of this sacred mountain.

86 Pima Mining District — To the west are waste dumps of copper mines that have been operating in the area since 1908. Here, under 200 feet of overburden, is one of the largest deposits of copper ore in the world. Nearly three million tons of copper have been removed from this mine. The huge main pit is more than 1,400 feet deep. The area is closed to traffic, but occasional tours are offered from about November through April. Go west on Duval Mine Road and follow signs to the visitor center, or call the Cyprus Sierrita Corporation for information.

77 Santa Rita Mountains — Directly to the east and running in a north-south direction for many miles are the towering Santa Rita Mountains. The highest point is Mount Wrightson at an elevation of 9,453 feet.

Exit 75 Sahuarita — Sahuarita, Spanish for "little saguaro cactus," was first a ranch, then a stage stop, and later a railroad station. Today this small community is the location of the Santa Cruz Valley Pecan Company and Pecan Store. Along the valley on the east side of the interstate is the world's largest pecan grove, covering more than 6,000 acres.

Exit 69 Titan Missile Museum — In an area known mostly for frontier history, an intercontinental missile might be unexpected. But that's what you will find at the Titan Missile Museum about a half-mile to the west on Duval Road. You can see the missile in its silo (all Titans were deactivated in 1982) and tour the control room, the crew's living quarters, and much more. Tours are offered daily. Modest admission fee.

Exit 65 Green Valley — A turnoff here will give you a chance to tour the retirement and leisure-living community of Green Valley. As a planned community, Green Valley provides a full slate of retail businesses and services, including a motel and several restaurants.

Exit 63 Continental and Madera Canyon — Near here, in 1914, the Continental Rubber Company established a plantation to experiment in producing rubber from the desert plant guayule. The experiment failed, so today Continental serves primarily as the gateway to Madera Canyon 13 miles down the paved road to the east. At Madera Canyon, in the vastness of the Santa Rita Mountains, you'll find campgrounds, the small Santa Rita Lodge, gorgeous scenery, hiking trails, and excellent bird-watching.

Exit 56 Elephant Head — Look to the east for a good view of Elephant Head, a massive intrusive rock formation created about 68 million years ago when molten rock from the earth's interior cooled.

This is also the exit to the Fred Lawrence Whipple Observatory's base camp and visitor center. The observatory, under the direction of the Smithsonian Institution, has its multiple mirror telescope, one of the world's largest, at the summit of Mount Hopkins (8,572 feet). To visit, exit east and go south on the frontage road to Elephant Head Road then turn east and follow the signs to the visitor center. Access is limited, but from March through November all-day bus tours (bring your own lunch) may be arranged by contacting Whipple Observatory, P.O. Box 97, Amado, AZ 85645-0097; telephone (602) 670-5707. There is a modest fee.

55 Canoa Ranch Rest Area — A pleasant roadside site with ramadas, picnic tables, and rest rooms awaits just south of this kilometer marker. Historically, this was a crossing point of the Santa Cruz River. As an original Mexican land grant, it was one of the earliest ranches in the valley.

Exit 48 Amado — The business district of this small community is just off the highway to the west. In addition to travelers' necessities, the stop also features the Cow Palace, a period restaurant and tavern established in the early 1900s.

47 Desert Grasslands — You have now left the cactus-studded lower Sonoran Desert and entered cooler, somewhat wetter, desert grasslands. Vegetation includes trees such as mesquite and scrub oak, plus other frost-tolerant plants.

Exit 34 Tubac and the Old Presidio — This is the site of the first European community in what became Arizona. Founded in 1752 as the Presidio (fort) of San Ignacio de Tubac, the location was thrice abandoned by protective garrisons and the general population. The third time, when American troops left for the Civil War, Apache raids drove settlers to safe haven in Tucson.

The area remained essentially deserted until recent decades. Tubac, the location for the first territorial newspaper, exists as a state historic park with an early church, frontier school house, and the remains of the old presidio. Fine artists' studios and galleries are located in the area, which also features several good restaurants and overnight accommodations.

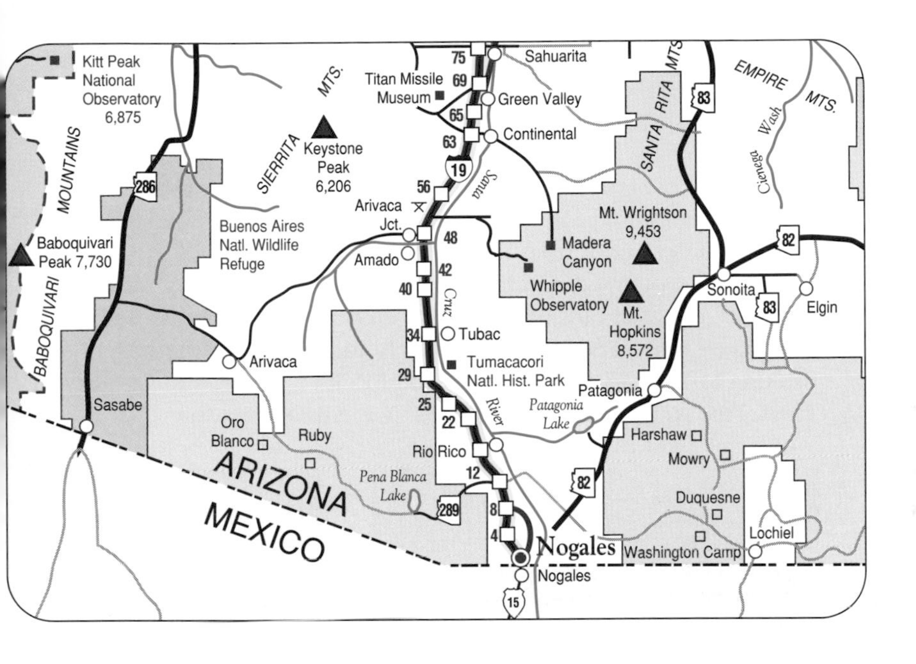

Exit 29 Tumacacori National Historical Park — Although Father Kino, the early Jesuit missionary, visited this area in 1691, the historic Mission of Tumacacori was not started until about 1800. Under pressure from Apache raiders, the mission was abandoned in 1841. It continued to deteriorate until 1908 when it was proclaimed a national monument. The museum is open daily for self-guided tours; a small entrance fee is charged. You may also visit the Santa Cruz Chili Factory with its small museum and store where all types of processed chili paste, sauce, and powder are sold.

Exit 17 Rio Rico — Calabasas (meaning pumpkin or gourd in Spanish) is the location near the Santa Cruz River where a Pima Indian village once stood. A small church was built in the area in 1797. By 1850 the site was a ranch with a huge adobe corral that covered four acres. For a time, Calabasas was a growing community. But by 1930 it was a ghost town and was plowed under and turned into farm land.

Today the planned community of Rio Rico, on the east side of the river, dots the hills and canyons around old Calabasas with handsome retirement and hideaway homes. At this same exit, looking to the west, you can see the Rio Rico Resort and Country Club. This sprawling hillside retreat is worth a short tour.

Exit 12 Peña Blanca Lake — State Route 289 leads 11 miles west of this exit to 52-acre Peña Blanca Lake. The lake offers a variety of game fish. Facilities include campgrounds, hiking trails, a small lodge, a restaurant, and boat rentals. Beyond the lake lie old back roads that wind past the once-prosperous gold mining areas of Ruby and Oro Blanco. A high-clearance vehicle is recommended for that road.

10 Pete Kitchen's Ranch — In the mid-1800s this area was extremely vulnerable to Apache attack. Nevertheless, it was here that Pete Kitchen built El Potrero, his fortified adobe ranch house on a hill near the confluence of Potrero Creek and the Santa Cruz River. From "Pete's Stronghold" he raised hogs and fought off Apache attacks for more than 14 years.

His partner, all of his neighbors, his stepson, and a number of ranch hands were killed by Apaches. It was said his hogs looked like four-legged pincushions from the Indian arrows. But all this only made Pete Kitchen more determined. The Apaches eventually gave up on him. He amassed a small fortune, then spent it generously over the years before dying peacefully among his many friends in Tucson. One tough and well-loved *hombre*.

Exit 8 Business Route to Nogales — Take this exit for a drive through downtown Nogales (Spanish for "walnuts," which grow here), Arizona, on your way to the international border. A popular stop on the American side is the Pimeria Alta Historical Society Museum on Grand Avenue, open every day of the week.

For a casual visit to the Mexican side of the border, it's best to park in the U.S. and walk across. There are a number of parking lots near the international line. No entry permit is required. The sightseeing, gift shops, and restaurants of Nogales, Sonora, draw large numbers of American tourists.

For more information on travel into Mexico, see Introduction, page 10.

FOR YOUR TRAVELING CONVENIENCE READ EACH MILEPOST BEFORE YOU GET THERE.

Starting Point — Your milepost trek starts in Flagstaff at the base of the soaring 12,643-foot San Francisco Mountains. For a brief profile of Flagstaff, turn to page 131. Your journey begins at Milepost 195 and proceeds in descending order to Milepost 0 at the California border.

Along the Way — This 195-mile westward trip on Interstate 40 drops in elevation from more than 7,000 feet near Flagstaff to less than 500 feet as you approach the Colorado River at Arizona's western border. For much of the trip, the modern highway follows three earlier historic roadways — old U.S. Route 66, the Atchison Topeka & Santa Fe Railroad, and Beale's frontier wagon road. The landscape will change from thick pine forests to harsh desert flatlands. If time permits, you can pause along the way to ride a 1910 steam train to the Grand Canyon, feed a "wild" burro in the ghost town of Oatman, or take a boat ride on Lake Havasu under the arches of London Bridge.

MILEPOST HIGHLIGHTS

Mount Elden — As you proceed west through Flagstaff, look directly north (3 o'clock position) for a view of Mount Elden, which rises to a height of 9,299 feet just north of the city. This volcanic center, about one million years old, exhibits a south face that is nearly solid rock with deep columnar joints caused by the rapid cooling of lava. A forest fire stripped most of the timber from Mount Elden in 1977.

(Left) The lofty San Francisco Peaks, glistening white in winter and blanketed green in the summer, are a majestic sight to passers-by.

193 San Francisco Mountains — As you proceed up the incline just ahead, you will get a clear view of the San Francisco Mountains directly to the north. Created by a series of volcanic eruptions about 2.8 million years ago, these magnificent peaks, generally covered with snow from fall through late spring, offer fine skiing. The highest point in the range (and in Arizona) is Humphrey's Peak at 12,643 feet. It is believed that the summit was originally above 15,000 feet, but a sideways explosion about 300,000 years ago and erosion have reduced its height.

189 Lava Fields of the Coconino Plateau — For the next 70 miles the broad plateau country west of the San Francisco Mountains is covered with ancient lava flows. A surface of soil developed over nearly 20,000 centuries covers much of the lava, but you will notice that lava is exposed in the road cuts along your route.

Exit 185 Navajo Army Depot — In early 1942, shortly after Pearl Harbor, the government created the Navajo Ordnance Depot near the small community of Bellemont. Adjacent to the Santa Fe Railroad, the installation stored, handled, and shipped ammunition and explosives. Most of the workers were from the Navajo reservation. To make them feel comfortable in their new surroundings, the Army built a Navajo "town," complete with traditional hogans (Navajo homes) and a trading post. More than 2,000 Native Americans worked at the site during World War II. Today, with a much smaller staff, the facility is operated by the Arizona National Guard.

184 Santa Fe Railroad — The tracks that parallel the highway much of the way belong to the Santa Fe Railroad and were built across Arizona in the early 1880s. The route was chosen for two reasons: It was the most easily traveled terrain and had reliable water sources for the steam engines.

183 Parks Rest Area — In a grove of tall pines is a rest stop with ramadas, picnic tables, and rest rooms.

Exit 178 Bill Williams Mountain — This exit takes you to the mostly residential community of Parks, so named for the park-like clearings in the forest. The 9,264-foot-tall cluster of volcanic domes (directly ahead)

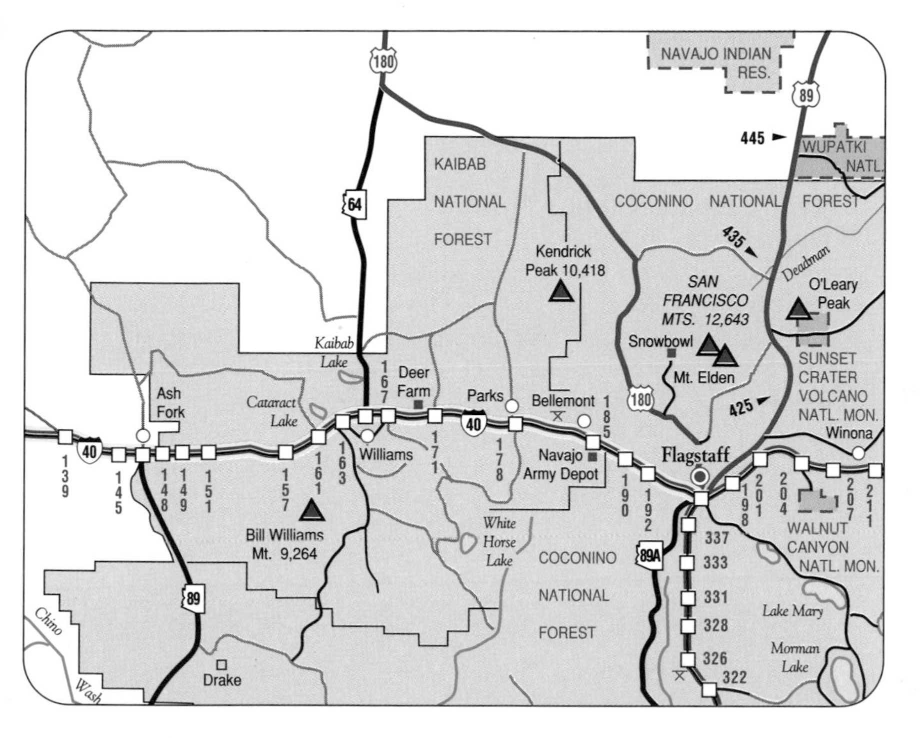

was named for one of Arizona's earliest and most colorful frontier characters. Bill Williams was an inveterate explorer and mountain man who wandered extensively through this region trapping beaver during the early 1800s. His life was filled with hair-raising adventures. His luck ran out in 1849 when he was attacked and killed by a Ute war party.

175 Ponderosa Pine Forest — At this milepost you are surrounded by a deep forest of ponderosa pine. Lumbering has been an important industry in this part of Arizona since the late 1800s. An uninterrupted stretch of this high-country timber continues for more than 200 miles to the southeast through the White Mountains and on into New Mexico, making it the largest stand of ponderosa pines in the United States. Most of the 19,000 square miles of Arizona forests (nearly twice the area of Vermont) are set aside as national forest.

173 Cinder Cone — To the south at this milepost (11 o'clock) is a low conical peak with a bare area that is a deep, rusty-red color. Under its foliage, the mountain, like many others in this area, is composed entirely of volcanic cinders. The Southwest's most spectacular cinder cone is Sunset Crater northeast of Flagstaff (see page 132).

Exit 171 Grand Canyon Deer Farm — This roadside stop features a petting zoo with deer, llamas, monkeys, peacocks, miniature donkeys, and other animals and birds. Admission is charged.

170 Beale's Wagon Road — In 1857 former Naval officer Edward Beale, traveling with an experimental pack train of 23 camels, moved across this area while forging a government-funded wagon road. The camels turned out to be ideal pack animals, but they scared the horses and mules. With the coming of the Civil War, the experiment was scrapped. Beale's route was followed by the railroads and the Arizona stretch of famous U.S. Route 66 (now State Route 66). Once called the "Main Street of America," old 66 was immortalized in the song and television show "Route 66." Today, much of Interstate 40 follows Beale's original route.

Exit 165 Williams — From this exit, State Route 64 runs north 63 miles to the South Rim of the Grand Canyon. Two miles north on this route, at Kaibab Lake, is a Forest Service campground for RVs and tents. Facilities include drinking water, grills, rest rooms, tables, and a boat ramp. Modest camping fee. Also at this exit, you can take a business loop into the community of Williams, which provides motels, restaurants, retail services, and tourist information. Williams is home to the Grand Canyon Railway, offering scheduled tours to the South Rim in old-fashioned steam trains. Call 1-800-THE-TRAIN for information.

Exit 161 Cataract Lake — About 1 mile north of the interstate is a small mountain lake named for nearby Cataract Creek. The creek flows north to the Grand Canyon and, in the spring or when it rains, has several small waterfalls along its course. The Forest Service campground has drinking water, fishing, and camp sites...but no cataracts. Closed from October to May. Modest camping fee.

160 Descending the Colorado Plateau — The northeastern third of Arizona lies on a vast highland area known as the Colorado Plateau. In some places the line of demarcation between this area and lower country is marked by steep cliffs. However in this region, the drop is more gradual. During the next 19 miles, you will descend 1,630 feet before reaching the community of Ash Fork. This elevation change also causes changes in local plant life. The ponderosa pines disappear west of exit 157 when you enter piñon pine and juniper country. Eastbound travelers, particularly truckers, are always glad when they reach the top of this long uphill climb.

Exit 146 Ash Fork — In the early days of the railroad, freighters hauled ore from Jerome north along Ash Creek then east to Williams. The freighters pressured the railroad for a closer shipping point, so the railroad built a siding where three forks of Ash Creek joined; thus the name Ash Fork. The location became an important cattle-shipping point with large stockyards.

Fred Harvey built the Escalante, one of his luxurious Harvey House facilities, along the railroad at Ash Fork. It was complete with elegant atmosphere, fine cuisine, and refined young Harvey Girls as waitresses. There was a shortage of single young women in Arizona in those days and the cowboys and railroad men patronized the Harvey Houses regularly. The Harvey Girls seldom remained single for long. It is said that half the male babies born in the West in those days were named either Fred or Harvey in honor of their parents' matchmaker.

This exit also provides access to State Route 89, which leads south to Prescott and Phoenix. Ash Fork offers motels, restaurants, and retail services.

Exit 139 Juniper Mountains — The distant mountains to the southwest at a 10 o'clock position are the Juniper Mountains, aptly named for the heavy growth of native juniper trees. At this point, Interstate 40 departs from old Route 66, with the earlier highway swinging north and west until the two again join in the community of Kingman.

132 Picacho Butte — To the south rises Picacho Butte. Every government survey along the 35th parallel passed near this point. Capt. Lorenzo Sitgreaves surveyed along the 35th parallel in 1851 to evaluate the land the United States had gained in the war with Mexico. From Picacho Butte, Sitgreaves continued nearly due west to the Colorado River.

This butte appears on Lt. Amiel Whipple's map from the 1853-54 survey for a transcontinental railroad route, but here his route turned south, eventually following the course of the Big Sandy River to the Bill Williams River and across the Colorado River.

Beale's wagon road, surveyed in 1857-58, and today's interstate and railroad also continue west to cross the Colorado at Needles, California.

Exit 128 Havasu Canyon — Beautiful Havasu Canyon on the Havasupai Indian Reservation is about 60 miles to the north, but there are no vantage points in the region accessible by auto. Havasu Canyon, with its spectacular waterfalls, blue green pools, and secluded setting, is often referred to as Shangri-La. It can be reached only by foot, horseback, or helicopter. Anyone entering the canyon must pay a modest fee to the Havasupai Indian Tribe and obtain advance permission to stay overnight on reservation property. Access to the Hilltop Trailhead is via State Route 66 and Indian Route 18.

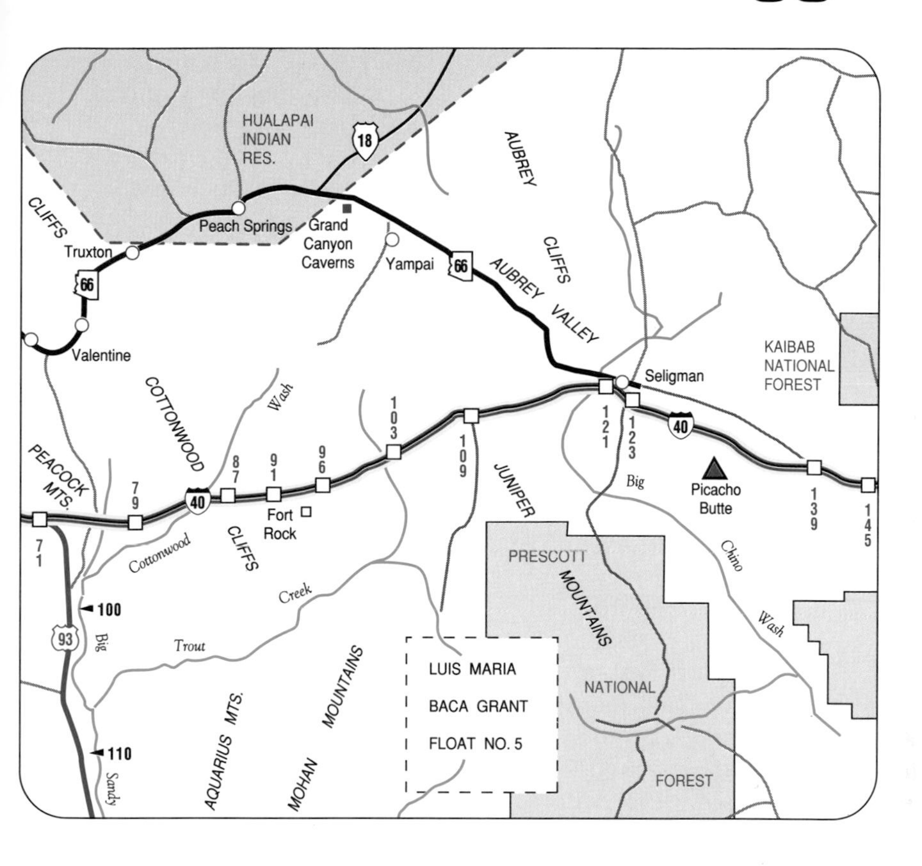

Exit 123 Seligman and the Land to the North — Seligman, an important railroad and highway stop in earlier years, was bypassed when Interstate 40 was built. This community of about 600 offers several motels and restaurants for travelers looking for a quiet place off the interstate. North of Seligman, the country is wild and lonely, with only two paved roads — State Route 66 and Indian Route 18 — in an area of several thousand square miles. The railroad leaves Interstate 40 at this point and parallels old 66.

120 Big Chino Wash — *Chino*, Spanish for "curly," describes the grama grass that flourishes in this long, wide valley that runs generally southeasterly almost to Prescott. The Big Chino Wash drains this valley and flows into the Verde River near its source above Paulden. Despite the verdant grasslands, early explorers found hard traveling in this region. Lack of dependable water resulted in little game to hunt and in long, dry marches. Cattle ranchers built stock tanks and today game is plentiful.

117 Aubrey Cliffs and Aubrey Valley — Directly north (4 o'clock position) are the Aubrey Cliffs and beyond them to the west, Aubrey Valley. Both are named for frontier explorer Francois X. Aubrey. Among his many exploits was an amazing horseback ride covering the 800 miles between Independence, Missouri, and Santa Fe, New Mexico, in five days and 13 hours. He discovered gold near the Colorado River and prospered in a freight and livestock business, but was stabbed to death in a Santa Fe saloon in 1854.

Exit 109 Baca Float Number 5 — This was part of a huge New Mexico land grant left to the heirs of Luis Maria Cabeza de Vaca by the Mexican government in 1821. Because of conflicting grants, the U.S. government allowed the family to "float" their choice of land in five grants of nearly 100,000 acres each in New Mexico and Arizona. Baca Float Number 5 is now a cattle ranch, encompassing part of the Juniper Mountains and the grasslands to the west.

100 Grand Canyon Caverns — Fifteen miles to the north, as the crow flies, tour guides escort visitors through the depths of the extensive dry caves of Grand Canyon Caverns. First explored in 1927, the caverns yielded the remains of a 20,000-year-old giant ground sloth perfectly preserved by the dry air.

94 Entering Mohave County — One of Arizona's four huge original counties, Mohave lost its northwest corner when Pah-Ute County was created in 1865. Nevada received Pah-Ute from Arizona in 1866 when it became a state. (At that time Nevada did not have enough people to become a state. It did, however, have vast deposits of gold and silver, which the Union needed to pay for the Civil War.) The county's citizens refused allegiance to Nevada for a time and continued to send representatives to Arizona. Arizona eventually gave up and the "lost" county became Clark County, Nevada, which contains Las Vegas.

Exit 91 Fort Rock Road — In 1866 Hualapai warriors attacked the stage stop southeast of this exit. Station master J.J. Buckman's son had constructed a rock playhouse at the site, and Buckman and another man leaped inside the small structure and traded shots with more than 50 marauders for many hours. The discouraged attackers finally left and Buckman changed the name of the station to Fort Rock to honor young Thad's playhouse.

The highway ahead winds through fields of rounded granite

boulders. They were originally part of an immense sheet of granite that cracked, forming rectangular-shaped blocks. These were assaulted from all sides by forces of erosion and have (after many millions of years) assumed their present rounded state.

Exit 87 **Aquarius Mountains, Cottonwood Cliffs** — The rugged country in this area is the meeting place of the Cottonwood Cliffs angling down from the north and the Aquarius Mountains coming in from the south. The Aquarius Mountains were named for the many streams flowing from them. Willow Creek, which runs down Cottonwood Wash, is lined with a thick growth of willows and cottonwoods. In summer months, a lush dome of greenery marks the course of the wash. Cottonwood Wash eventually joins the Big Sandy River to the west.

Exit 71 **Peacock Mountains** — At this point, U.S. Route 93 from Phoenix intersects with Interstate 40. To the north (2 o'clock) are the Peacock Mountains. The name has nothing to do with brightly feathered birds. In 1857 Lt. Joseph C. Ives (the first white man to descend to the bottom of the Grand Canyon) was leading a party through this region. The men and mules, having gone without water for days, were suffering from intense thirst. G.H. Peacock, a member of the expedition, located a bubbling spring in a deep ravine. As a gesture of gratitude, the spring and the surrounding mountains were named for him.

64 **Hualapai Mountains and Grand Wash Cliffs** — Directly to the south (9 o'clock position) are the rugged Hualapai Mountains, 8,417 feet at their highest point. Hualapai Valley is the broad plain extending for many miles to the north. Old Route 66 angles across this valley in a southwesterly direction to rejoin Interstate 40 in Kingman.

The high cliffs on the far northeast side of Hualapai Valley (3 o'clock position) are the Grand Wash Cliffs. They mark the southwest edge of the vast Colorado Plateau, which curves more than 350 miles across Arizona and into New Mexico. This lip of the Colorado Plateau is known along its course in Arizona by various names, including the Grand Wash Cliffs, Cottonwood Cliffs, Sycamore Canyon, Oak Creek Canyon, Mogollon Rim, and White Mountains. In New Mexico they become the Mogollon Mountains.

Exit 53 Kingman, Cerbat Mountains — The mountains directly ahead that angle to the north are the Cerbats, from the Coco-Mohave Indian word for bighorn sheep. Rich in gold, silver, and other minerals, the Cerbats swarmed with miners during the last decades of the previous century. But today, frontier boom towns like Cerbat, Stockton Hill, and Mineral Park are only crumbling memories. This exit leads to the commercial district of Kingman.

Exit 48 Kingman Historic District — Kingman began as a railroad and mining town in 1880. Present-day Kingman, at the junction with U.S. 93 (north to Lake Mead and Las Vegas), bustles as a stopping point for travelers heading in all directions. Clark Gable and Carole Lombard were married in a small Kingman church. The community's main thoroughfare is named for character actor and favorite-son Andy Devine. The Mojave County Museum (east at Exit 48) is worth a visit.

Exit 44 Road to Oatman — Seen from this exit, the high desert mountains to the west that stretch both north and south are the Black Mountains. Dark and extremely rugged, they effectively blocked most frontier travel for a distance of more than 100 miles. The Colorado River flows just the other side of the mountains. Sacramento Valley, through which you are now

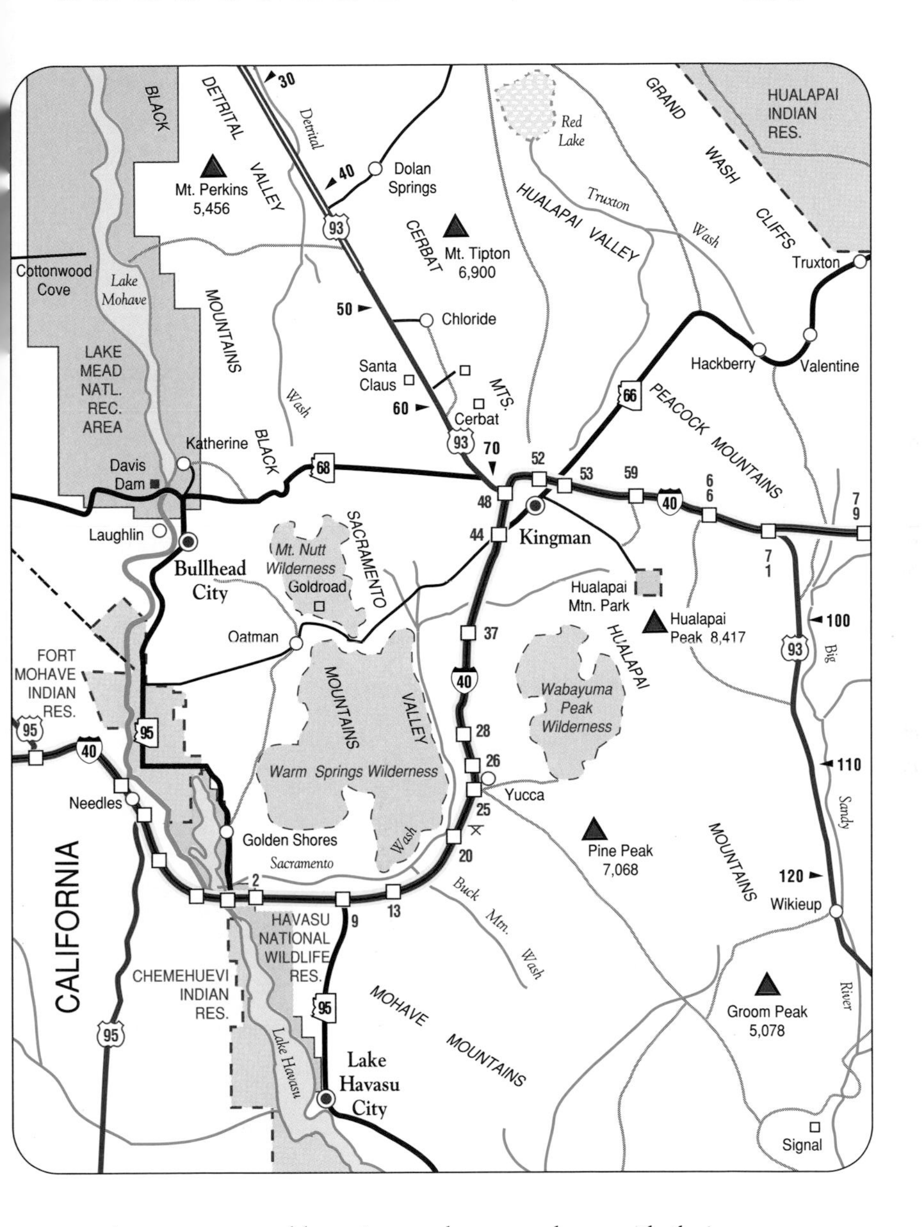

passing, was named by miners who came here with their California regiments in 1863.

At this exit, old Route 66 angles off to the southwest on its way to Gold Road and Oatman, 24 miles to the west. Oatman, originally named Vivian, blossomed as a mining community when a rich vein of ore was discovered in 1902. In three years the local mines produced more than $3 million in gold. Prosperous times lasted until the '30s. Today, the ghost town of Oatman is a tourist attraction where wild burros wander in from the hills to mooch handouts from passersby. Gold Road, a real ghost town, provides an interesting drive as the road zig-zags through the mine-pocked canyon.

Exit 26 **Yucca** — The railroad established Yucca, named for the yucca plants in the area. The station grew into a small settlement that served the mines in the area. Today it is the site of the Ford Motor Company's Desert Proving Ground.

24 **Joshua Trees** — Joshua trees, which grow in abundance in this area, were named by early Mormon settlers because their arms were raised toward the heavens in supplication, similar to the traditional pose of the Biblical Joshua. Joshua trees, and other yucca plants, are not cactus, but members of the lily family. Most yucca have a single trunk with a large rosette of long, pointed leaves at the top. The Joshua tree, however, is many-armed with a shorter rosette of leaves at the end of each appendage. Very old specimens develop a tree-like bark.

23 **Haviland Rest Area** — Includes rest rooms, handicapped facilities, drinking water, a telephone, and ramadas.

15 **Smoke thorns** — In the washes between the roadways Smoke thorns (locally called smoke trees) can be seen in abundance. A frost-sensitive plant, smoke thorns are uncommon in Arizona except in the westernmost part of the state. The name originates from the gray-green, plume-like vegetation which resembles campfire smoke in a desert wash. In May or June beautiful purple flowers enhance the illusion.

Exit 9 Route to Lake Havasu City — Twenty miles to the south on State Route 95 is Lake Havasu City. In 1963 industrialist Robert P. McCulloch started a planned community for his employees in a lonely part of the Arizona desert that had been called Site 6, a World War II rest and recuperation installation and gravel landing strip for student-pilot practice.

More than 20,000 people call the area home, while countless boating and fishing enthusiasts visit year-round. The area's leading attraction is the authentic London Bridge, which was purchased by McCulloch in 1968. The historic structure of more than 10,000 tons was dismantled, each stone numbered, shipped to the Arizona desert, and reassembled over a newly created arm of Lake Havasu.

1 Geographic Contrast — Just south of the highway near this milepost the sand and gravel of broad Mojave Valley stretching down from the north meets the wildly tossed formations of an area of ancient volcanic activity. The Needles, for which Needles, California, is named, are actually volcanic formations in the mountains on the Arizona side of the river.

0 Colorado River, California Border — At this point, the mighty Colorado flows languidly. Its waters, backed up by Parker Dam about 40 miles downstream, form Lake Havasu. Upstream, Davis, Hoover, and Glen Canyon dams have harnessed the energy of this great river, providing electrical power and irrigation water to vast areas of Arizona and California. Both the city of Los Angeles and the Central Arizona Project siphon water into huge aqueducts from Lake Havasu.

Jagged rock formations of the needles along the Colorado River in Havasu National Wildlife Refuge. DAVID ELMS, JR.

TOUR PHOTOGRAPHS BY JAMES TALLON

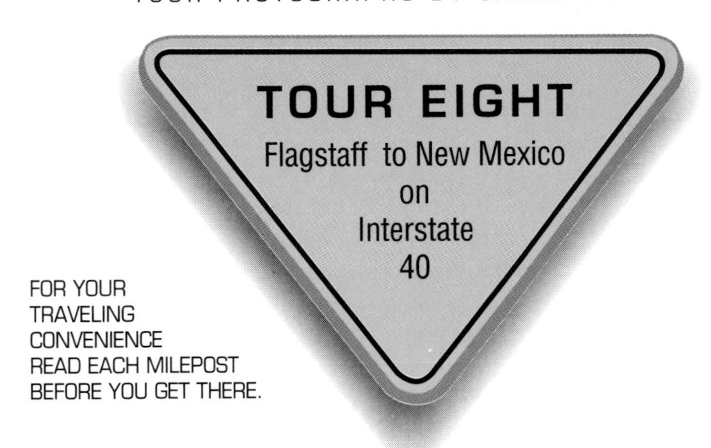

FOR YOUR TRAVELING CONVENIENCE READ EACH MILEPOST BEFORE YOU GET THERE.

Starting Point — Your tour starts in Flagstaff at the base of the soaring 12,643-foot San Francisco Mountains. Interstate exit numbers and mileposts are in ascending order. For a brief profile of Flagstaff, turn to page 131.

Along the Way — This 165-mile trip begins in heavily forested pine country, then moves eastward through old lava fields. Farther east, the lava is replaced by rolling grasslands. Then, nearing the New Mexico border, you enter a region of sandstone cliffs. For much of your journey, the land to the north reveals the barren dunes of the Painted Desert. To the south, the forested slopes of the White Mountains stand against the sky.

This is also a route rich in history and cultural diversity, a land where ancient civilizations flourished and disappeared, where frontier ruffians clashed with steel-nerved lawmen, where hardy Mormon pioneers challenged the harsh land and created settlements that endure to this day. It is also a land of stark beauty, immense sky, and endless distance.

MILEPOST HIGHLIGHTS

San Francisco Mountains — As you proceed east through Flagstaff, look directly north for a view of Arizona's highest point, 12,643-foot Humphreys Peak in the pine- and aspen-clad San Francisco Mountains. Formed by volcanic eruptions about 2.8 million years ago, this impressive mountain range offers terrific downhill and cross-country skiing.

(Left) In 1924 Fred Harvey built the Painted Desert Inn. Today, located north of Exit 311 and converted into a museum, it houses the world's earliest datable dinosaur. Dinosaurs first stamped the Earth 225 million years ago.

199 Mount Elden — Immediately north, the bulk of Mount Elden (elevation 9,299 feet) stands between the city and the San Francisco Mountains. This volcanic center, about 1 million years old, exhibits a south face that is nearly solid rock with deep columnar joints caused by the rapid cooling of lava. In 1977 a forest fire stripped most of the timber off the slopes.

Exit 201 To U.S. Route 89 — Twelve miles north on U.S. 89 is the entrance to Sunset Crater Volcano National Monument and the extensive prehistoric ruins of Wupatki National Monument (modest entry fee). Beyond this milepost, just north of the highway, are reddish volcanic cones where cinders are quarried. This hard, porous material is widely used in Arizona highway construction.

Exit 204 Walnut Canyon National Monument — This deep limestone canyon holds the remains of more than 300 prehistoric cliff dwellings. The visitors center offers exhibits and artifacts of the Sinagua culture, which mysteriously disappeared

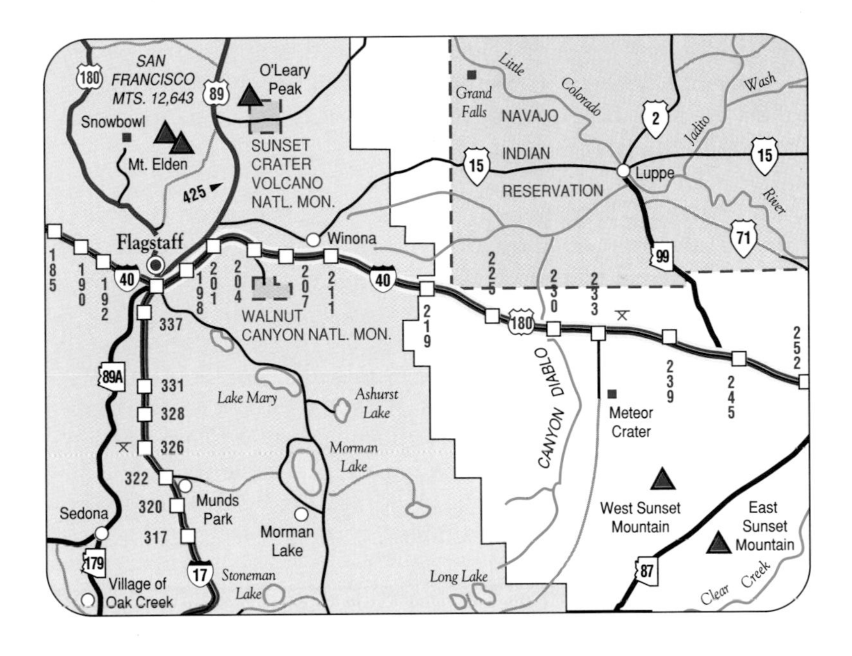

about 700 years ago. More than 100 stairs and a paved walking trail descend the steep canyon and provide a tour of the site (modest entry fee).

Exit 207 **View of Sunset Crater** — For an impressive view of Sunset Crater, exit at this point and proceed to the service-road stop sign. Directly north stands the black volcanic cone with its rim of red cinders. Formed about A.D. 1065, this young volcano reaches an elevation of 8,000 feet. Because of its moon-like composition, the area around the crater was used as a training site for Apollo astronauts and their moon-roving vehicle.

Exit 211 **Winona** — The tiny community of Winona gained a measure of fame when it was included in the lyrics of the song "Route 66." Old 66 has been replaced by Interstate 40, but the lyrics linger: "Flagstaff, Arizona, don't forget Winona, Kingman, Barstow, San Bernardino...." Also at this exit you can see where railroad engineers are excavating cinders from a cinder cone for track maintenance.

216 **Plateau Country and Cinder Cones** — Trees in this region will be primarily piñon pine and juniper, but often the countryside is covered only with grass. To the north, accumulations of ash and cinders around volcanic vents created five prominent cinder cones. Volcano country ends just a few miles

ahead. You will continue across a bed of Kaibab limestone.

At about Milepost 230, the limestone will become overlaid by sandstone formations (principally red) that continue to appear all the way to the New Mexico border.

218 Padre Canyon — Ten miles ahead is Canyon Diablo (Devil's Canyon), which once served as a hideout for bandits and ruffians. It is said that Padre Canyon was given its priestly name to offset Canyon Diablo's connotation of evil.

220 Navajo Reservation — At this milepost the southwest corner of the vast Navajo Indian Reservation almost touches the highway. From this point, tribal land stretches north and east for more than 25,000 square miles. Almost in the center of the Navajo Reservation is the smaller Hopi Indian Reservation, which covers several thousand square miles.

222 Mogollon Rim — The blue ridges at the southern horizon are part of the Mogollon Rim where the Colorado Plateau drops down to the lower basins and ranges of central Arizona. The cliffs, sometimes 2,000 feet high, run across Arizona in a northwest-southeast direction for nearly 200 miles. At an elevation of 7,000 feet, the Rim's climate is much like that of Flagstaff. The wide band of forest that blankets the Rim is part of the world's largest stand of ponderosa pine.

Exit 225 Buffalo Range Road — A small buffalo herd (American bison) grazes on a fenced range 11 miles to the south. You won't see any of the shaggy animals from the interstate, but, as you proceed east, you might get a glimpse of wild pronghorn. Resembling antelope, these buff-colored mammals with pronged horns are among the fastest runners on the continent. They have been clocked at more than 60 miles per hour.

Exit 230 Canyon Diablo and Two Guns — In 1857 Lt. Edward Beale was locating an east-west wagon road through this region. This canyon presented such an obstacle that he had to detour 40 miles to get around it. His map names it Canyon Diablo. Three miles north of this bridge are the remnants of a deserted town of the same name. In the late 1800s, the town was said to hold the meanest collection of lowlifes in the West.

Two Guns, just to the south of the interstate (where remains of old rock buildings still stand) was also rough. "Two Gun" Miller opened a store in the vicinity and named the area Two Guns. A man foolish enough to open a competing establishment was shot to death by Miller, but a jury ruled it was self-defense. Miller lived in a cave in the canyon and terrorized archaeologists who came looking for ancient artifacts. Tough country!

Exit 233 **Meteor Crater** — Six miles south, a huge hole in the ground, 570 feet deep and nearly a mile across, was created about 49,000 years ago when a meteor nearly 100 feet in diameter smashed into the earth. This is another place where, because of its moon-like surface, NASA has tested equipment and trained astronauts. Meteor Crater is privately owned. An entrance fee is charged to view the exhibits and walk the crater's rim.

235 **Meteor Crater Rest Area** — Beyond this milepost is a roadside rest area with ramadas, picnic tables, and rest rooms.

Exit 245 **Leupp and Chevelon Butte** — The small Navajo community of Leupp, named for Francis E. Leupp, U.S. Commissioner of Indian affairs from 1905-1908, is a tribal subagency 15 miles to the north. The Navajos call the place *Tsiizizi*, which means "scalps." Some say an Indian fight that included scalping was fought here. But others claim that a former government agent with a toupee was the inspiration.

To the south are several prominent buttes. Farthest east is Chevelon Butte, named for an 1850s trapper who accidentally poisoned himself by eating wild parsnips. The unfortunate diner receives further recognition with Chevelon Canyon, Chevelon Lake, Chevelon Wildlife Area, and Chevelon Crossing.

Exit 252 **Winslow** — Winslow got its start as a railroad terminal named after Gen. Edward F. Winslow. Today, with nearly 10,000 automobiles a day passing by on Interstate 40, Winslow does a brisk business offering motels, restaurants, and services to the tourist trade.

Exit 257 **Homolovi Ruins State Park** — This exit leads 1 mile north to the turnoff to Homolovi Ruins State Park, the site of four pueblo villages. Occupied between A.D. 1250 and A.D. 1450 by the ancient Anasazi people, ancestors of the Hopi

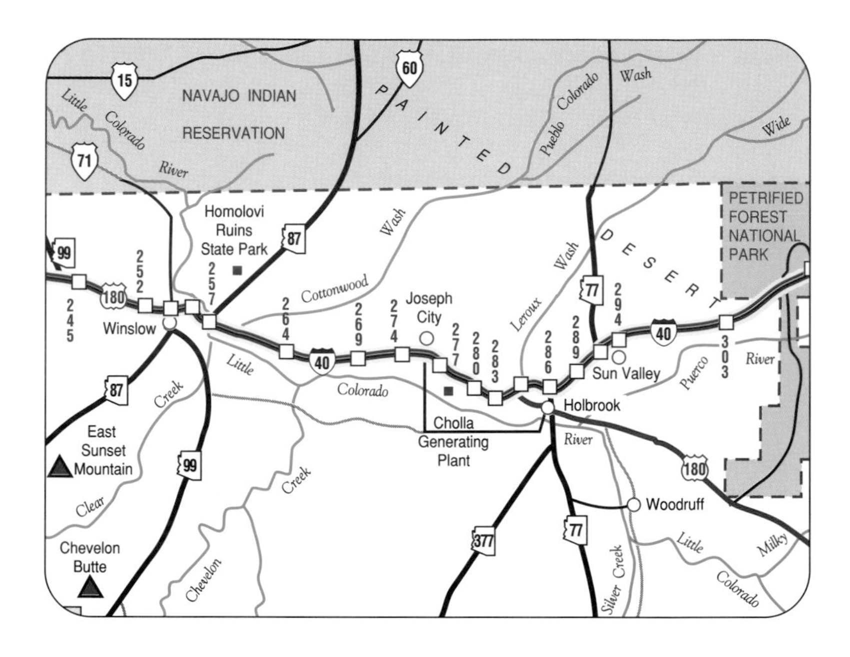

Indians, *Homolovi* is Hopi for "place of the mounds." State Route 87, accessible from this exit, is the most comfortable and direct route to the Hopi mesa-top villages about 60 miles north.

258 **Sunset Crossing** — On the Little Colorado River to the south, the sandstone bottom provided one of the few good early-day crossings of this unpredictable river. It was used by Lieutenant Beale in 1858, the Wheeler expedition in the 1870s, and countless immigrants from Utah who settled in central and southern Arizona. The name comes from Sunset Pass (between East Sunset and West Sunset mountains), a major landmark on the trail 20 miles southwest from here.

Exit 264 **Chevelon Creek** — This dependable stream flows north from the Mogollon Rim country. In the mid-1800s trappers found it filled with otter and beaver. It is named for the same Chevelon as Chevelon Butte (see Exit 245).

Exit 274 **Joseph City** — This quiet farm community, founded in 1876 by Mormon settlers who named it for their prophet Joseph Smith, straddles a remnant of old U.S. Route 66. The first building in the area was a small fort of mud and logs. Surviving as the oldest settlement in Navajo County, Joseph City has no business district and is reminiscent of early, rural America.

Exit 277 Cholla Generating Plant — The massive electrical generating plant on the south side of the interstate runs on coal that is strip-mined on the Navajo Reservation. The tribe's vast reserves contribute nearly $30 million annually to the Navajo treasury.

Nearby is Cholla Lake County Park with ramadas, picnic tables, RV hookups, showers, campgrounds, and boat launching facilities — a nice place for a picnic or an overnight stay (modest fee).

Exit 283 Hashknife Cattle Country — In the late 1800s, the vast holdings of the Aztec Land & Cattle Company extended south and west from this point over more than 2 million acres of knee-deep grassland. Called the Hashknife outfit because its brand resembled that utensil, the ranch employed more than a few outlaws and rough characters. Drought and overgrazing brought the enterprise to an end in 1902. The thick grass never returned, but today, with better range management, ranching is still an important industry in northern Arizona.

Arizona Historical Society

Exit 286 Holbrook — Once an important way station on the railroad and old Route 66, Holbrook now serves tourists and the ranching industry.

One of the West's most celebrated gunfights took place in Holbrook in 1887. Sheriff Commodore Perry Owens (Commodore was his first name), a dashing character with hair below his shoulders, single-handedly engaged the notorious Cooper-Blevins gang, killing three and wounding one in a matter of moments. Holbrook's Navajo County Museum chronicles this famous gunfight and all of the area's colorful history.

The Cooper-Blevins gang was involved in the Pleasant Valley War. (For more about the war see Chapter 12, Milepost 284 — Road to Young, page 162.)

Exit 292 Painted Desert — Look to the north for a view of the Painted Desert — thousands of miles of multicolored dunes with almost no vegetation. State Route 77 is another paved route to the Hopi mesas where Oraibi endures as the oldest continuously inhabited community in the United States. The Hopi have lived there for more than 900 years, and their ancestors, the Anasazi, inhabited the area for a thousand years before that.

297 **White Mountains** — From this point, on a clear day (and most days are), you can look south 80 miles to the far horizon where Arizona's heavily forested White Mountains stand against the sky. The tallest peak, Mount Baldy, is 11,590 feet high and often displays snow even during warmer months. Apaches hold the mountain sacred, and (by law) only tribal members are permitted on its summit.

300 **Little Lithodendron Wash** — While conducting a survey through this area in 1853, Lt. Amiel W. Whipple named many of the local landmarks, including this usually dry wash. Not a scientific term, the word "lithodendron" sprang from Whipple's scholarly background. He simply combined litho, meaning stone, with dendron, meaning tree-like. He was obviously referring to the numerous petrified logs in the area. Big Lithodendron Wash is just beyond Milepost 303.

Exit 303 **Adamana** — This tiny settlement, named for sheep rancher Adam Hanna, was the rail station where early tourists began their trip to the Petrified Forest and on to the Painted Desert. Fred Harvey touring cars picked up adventurous travelers and transported them overland through these wonders of the world before returning them to the train. Their next stop was usually Williams, 30 miles west of Flagstaff, where they would change trains and head to the Grand Canyon.

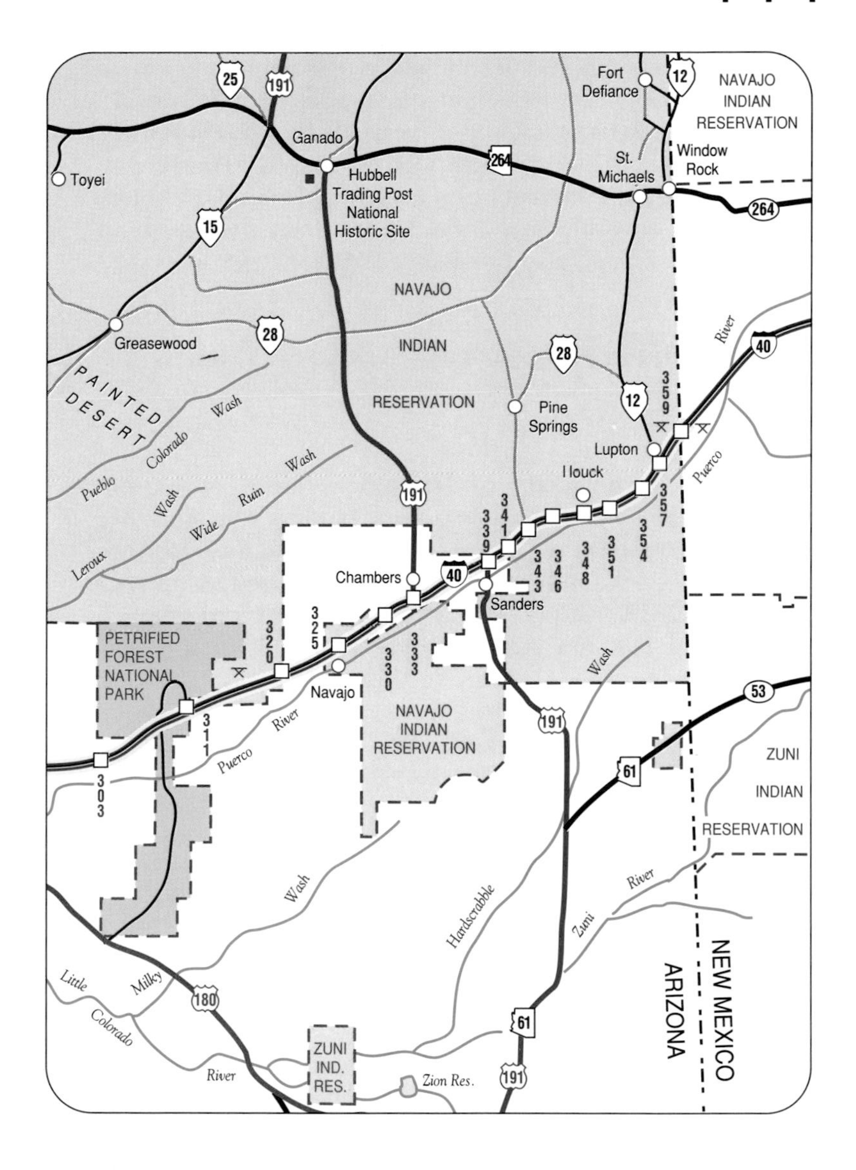

Exit 311 Petrified Forest National Park — On both sides of Interstate 40 is an intriguing geological "open book" of the earth's distant past. The world's oldest dinosaur was unearthed here in 1985.

The area is composed of stratified, multicolored hills where ancient life-forms and fallen tree trunks have been frozen in stone for hundreds of millions of years. The park (modest fee) offers a 28-mile scenic drive through the Petrified Forest.

The park's museum features a fossilized dinosaur and offers exhibits that cover the region from Triassic times to the era of early man. The park also provides a restaurant, gift shop, and service station.

315 **Roadside Rest Area** — Beyond this milepost is a parking area with shade trees and picnic tables, but no rest rooms.

Exit 325 **Community of Navajo** — Navajo, as you can see, never developed much as a town, but it *is* an historic site. In a driving snowstorm on December 29, 1863, John Goodwin, having entered the new territory by wagon, raised an American flag and took the oath of office as Arizona's first territorial governor. An historical marker beside the service road provides more information.

Exit 333 **U.S. Route 191** — This exit is a popular entry point to the Navajo Reservation. U.S. 191 leads to the community of Ganado and the Hubbell Trading Post. Developed in 1878, the still-operating trading post is now a National Historic Site with a visitors center, exhibits, and picnic areas. Farther north is the magnificence of Canyon de Chelly National Monument and its impressive prehistoric cliff dwellings.

340 **Enter Navajo Indian Reservation** — Twice, miles back, you crossed jutting corners of the Navajo Reservation, but from this point to the New Mexico border, your route will be entirely across tribal land.

Exit 348 **Houck** — Originally the Santa Fe Railroad's third station west of the New Mexico Line, Houck was named for James D. Houck, a sheep rancher and trading post operator here from 1877 to 1885. Houck was also a member of the Arizona legislature and a sheriff's deputy. The Navajo called the area around this exit Coyote Water.

As a deputy, Houck was involved in the Pleasant Valley War and the lynching on the Mogollon Rim of James Stott, James Scott, and Billy Wilson. (For more about the lynchings see Tour 12, Milepost 312 — Pleasant Valley War, page 163.) Houck committed suicide in Cave Creek, near Phoenix, in 1921.

356 **Sandstone Cliff Formations** — Soaring sandstone cliffs — formed from 60 to 200 million years ago — typify the stark, lonely beauty of the Indian country to the north. Auto travel on the reservation is safe on paved roads. Tribal police patrol and offer assistance, and motels, restaurants, and other services are available in major communities.

Exit 357 **Navajo Route 12** — This access to the Navajo Reservation leads north 27 miles to Window Rock, tribal capital of the Navajo Nation. Named for a huge eroded hole in a rock wall nearby, the community serves as a gateway to the scenic wonders of the reservation. Window Rock offers the Navajo Tribal Museum, a zoological park, picnic grounds (just beneath the window), campgrounds, a motel, restaurants, and shopping. For travel information call or visit the Navajo Department of Tourism in Window Rock.

Exit 359 **Entering New Mexico** — This area is known as Painted Cliffs. Beyond this milepost, your Arizona trek on Interstate 40 ends. Just across the border, New Mexico welcomes you with a pleasant roadside rest area.

TOUR PHOTOGRAPHS BY DAVID ELMS, JR.

FOR YOUR TRAVELING CONVENIENCE READ EACH MILEPOST BEFORE YOU GET THERE.

Starting Point — Your journey starts in Phoenix, the capital of Arizona. For a brief profile of Phoenix, turn to page 27.

Along the Way — This tour of approximately 250 miles angles steadily northwest from the Phoenix area and ends at Hoover Dam, one of the world's most impressive engineering feats. Standing 726 feet above bedrock, the dam required 3.25 million cubic feet of concrete. Its construction claimed the lives of 96 workers. Lake Mead, impounded behind the dam, is America's largest man-made lake.

Much of this trek passes through sparsely populated country but offers rapidly changing geography that ranges from desert flatlands to soaring, distant mountain ranges. You will drive through one of the Southwest's most impressive Joshua tree forests and cross badlands traversed by the Spanish conquistadors on their ill-fated search for gold. You will skirt mountains that, 110 years ago, were the site of one of the West's busiest mining regions, and get a bird's-eye view of the mighty Colorado River at the bottom of the canyon it has been carving out of rock for more than 5 million years.

MILEPOST HIGHLIGHTS

Note: Proceeding northwest from Phoenix to Wickenburg on U.S. Route 60, the mileposts will be in descending order. Because three U.S. highways overlap on your route to Lake Mead, the milepost sequencing will change at Wickenburg and Kingman. The narrative will inform you of the change when it occurs.

(Left) Willow Beach on the Colorado River, as seen from the scenic overlook along U.S. Route 93 at Milepost 13.

The Community of Surprise — Your tour starts beyond the western limits of Phoenix on U.S. Route 60 approaching Surprise. Today metropolitan Phoenix is closing in on Surprise, but when it was established in 1938, it was in an isolated area. In those days it was a surprise to find even a small community in such a lonely setting — thus the name.

141 **Sun City West** — Directly east, and accessed by Meeker Boulevard, is Sun City West, a retirement community developed by the Del Webb Corp. Sun City West and Sun City (6 miles southeast) have a combined golden-years population of nearly 66,000.

136 **Luke Air Force Base Auxiliary Field** — The USAF operates an auxiliary field near here (Luke AFB is farther south), but the real show is in the sky where F-15 Eagles and other jet fighters roar by on training runs.

134 **White Tank Mountains** — To the south Maricopa County operates White Tank Desert Mountain Park, which features picnic ramadas, a campground, and miles of scenic desert hiking trails. In this land of little rain, the White Tanks are named for several rock basins of light-coated granite that hold water long after the infrequent rains have gone. These ideal water holes for wildlife were also known to prehistoric Hohokam Indians. The Hohokam scratched numerous abstract and animal petroglyphs on rocks along the trail to the tanks.

132 **Central Arizona Project Aqueduct** — Beyond this milepost, you pass over the Central Arizona Project Aqueduct. This 330-mile canal has a capacity to carry nearly 2 billion gallons of water per day from the Colorado River to delivery points in central and southern Arizona.

131 **Lower Sonoran Vegetation** — The trees growing in this area of the lower Sonoran Desert are mesquite (with rough dark bark) and paloverde (smooth bark, green limbs). *Paloverde*, translated from Spanish, means "green stick."

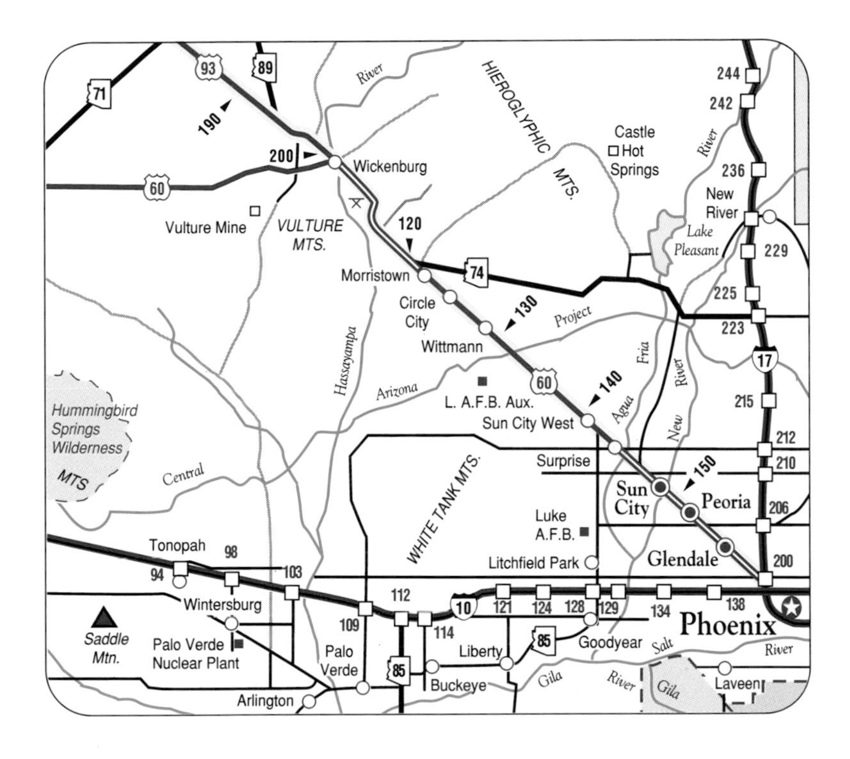

129 The Community of Wittmann — Beyond this milepost, you will pass through Wittmann. As early as 1920 it was called Nada, which in Spanish means "nothing." Later, to honor the man who financed the construction of a nearby irrigation dam, the name was changed to Wittmann.

In 1886 Barney Martin, his wife, and three children were killed near here in a holdup and robbery. The villains, believed to be the Valenzuela gang, escaped when the posse lost their trail. One member of the gang was later tracked and killed, for another murder, by a posse near Gila Bend. The others escaped to Mexico.

126 Saguaro Cactus — Many saguaros appear on both sides of the highway. They are the identifying plant of the Sonoran Desert. More than 90 miles north, beyond Wikieup, they disappear in the transition to the Mohave Desert.

121 Morristown — Established in 1897 to serve as a railroad siding for the Vulture Mine, Morristown later became the stop for passengers continuing east by stage to enjoy the elegant accommodations and soothing mineral waters of Castle Hot Springs. Today Morristown, the Vulture Mine, and Castle Hot Springs are very quiet.

116 Hassayampa River Preserve Rest Area — Along the course of the Hassayampa River, just west of the highway, the Nature Conservancy maintains a forest of cottonwood trees that serves as a sanctuary for nearly 230 species of wild birds. The site provides rest rooms, picnic tables, and walking paths. Access to the Nature Conservancy itself is at Milepost 114.

112 Entering Wickenburg — Wickenburg is known for its guest ranches and easygoing lifestyle. Back in 1863, it emerged as a boom town, created by Henry Wickenburg's nearby discovery of gold. The rugged mountains to the southwest are the location of the Vulture Mine. The mine (named for circling buzzards) was one of the richest in Arizona history, but the area was mined out by 1942 and operations ceased.

111 Hassayampa River and Wishing Well — The river's name, supposedly of Indian origin, is said to mean "river upside down," because Hassayampa's waters run mostly underground. On the west bank a small park with a wishing well and drinking fountain beckons to travelers. However, be warned! Legend claims that those who drink from the Hassayampa never tell the truth again. (Is the legend lying about lying...hmmm?)

West of the river, proceed through downtown Wickenburg, turning north on Tegner Street, which becomes U.S. Route 93 to Kingman and Lake Mead. U.S. Route 60, which has been the principal route since Phoenix, now turns west toward the California border.

(Note: Milepost sequencing changes to that of U.S. Route 93. It begins at Milepost 200 and continues in descending order.)

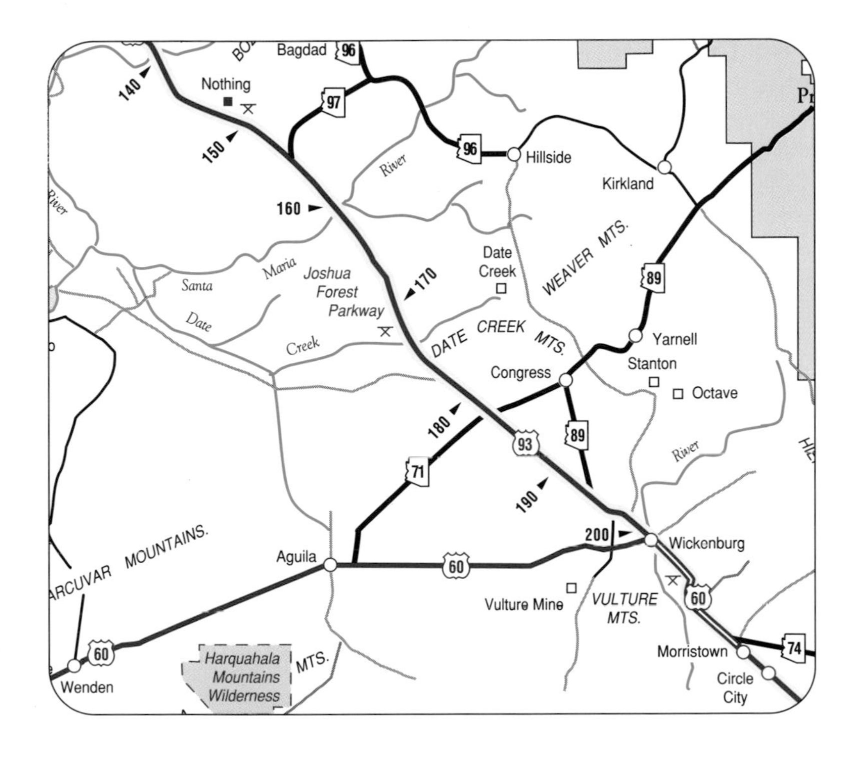

197 Vulture Mine Turnoff — Just past this milepost the Vulture Mine Road leads to the historic Vulture Mine, which has been well-preserved and, as of this printing, is occasionally open to the public. Admission is charged.

194 Junction with State Route 89 — Beyond this milepost a paved highway to the northeast follows a scenic route through mining and ranching country past the ghost towns of Stanton and Octave to the old territorial capital of Prescott.

Charles P. Stanton, for whom the ghost town is named, owned a store but had two competitors, Yaqui Wilson and William Partridge. Stanton incited a feud between the men but, when Partridge killed Wilson and went to jail, a silent partner named Timmerman appeared. Subsequently, Timmerman sold the operation to Barney Martin. Frustrated, Stanton then hired a local desperado, Francisco Vega, to kill both of them. Vega first murdered Timmerman, then bushwhacked Martin and his family.

Later that year justice was served when one of Vega's men, Christo Lucero, gunned Stanton down for insulting Lucero's sister. Not a lot of tears were shed for Stanton, but the town retained his name, boomed in the 1890s, then faded into a ghost.

191 Creosote Bushes — The low-growing, dull-green shrubs, abundant on both sides of the highway, are creosote bushes. It is believed by some scientists that these plants may be the oldest living things on earth. Some specimens may be nearly 12,000 years old. A central plant sends out runners that pop up as extensions of the original. These send out more runners and more extensions shoot up. What appears to be many creosote bushes may actually be only one plant. The process continues through the centuries.

187 Date Creek and Weaver Mountains — In the near distance and at about the 2 o'clock position, the Date Creek Mountains rise above Date Creek. No dates ever grew there, but *datal* did. That's what the Mexicans in the area called the fruit of the prickly pear cactus. Early Anglo settlers corrupted datal to "date."

The taller peaks beyond are the Weaver Mountains, named for the famed 19th-century Arizona trailblazer and gold prospector Paul Weaver. Weaver's nickname, "Paulino," was eventually twisted into Pauline. Weaver generally wore a pair of pistols, but there is no record of him ever drawing on anyone who called him Pauline.

183 Junction with State Route 71 — To the northeast, the road passes the site of the once-flourishing mining town of Congress. Before the turn of the century, the fabulously rich Congress Mine employed more than 400 men. By the 1930s, the mine was worked out and Congress joined the growing list of Arizona ghost towns.

177 Joshua Forest Parkway — This region contains one of the Southwest's most impressive stands of Joshua trees, the largest member of the yucca family. Joshua trees are an identifying plant of the Mohave Desert, which extends into western Arizona. Like all yucca plants, the Joshua tree cannot pollinate itself. Its continuation has always depended on the tiny *pronuba moth* that purposefully gathers and carries yucca pollen from plant to plant. The moth's larvae, in turn, feed off the yucca fruit, which, of course, wouldn't develop unless mother moth helped with the pollination — an outstanding example of plant/insect interdependence.

173 Rest Area — Beyond this milepost is a roadside stop with a picnic table and ramada, but no rest rooms. It's a good place to stretch your legs and take a closer look at the Joshua trees.

161 Santa Maria River — Leaving Joshua Forest Parkway you will cross the Santa Maria River. A mere trickle most of the time, the Santa Maria runs at flood levels during heavy rains. In 1604, the Spanish explorer Juan de Oñate followed the Santa Maria west to the Colorado River on his unsuccessful quest for legendary lost mines of silver and gold.

156 State Route 97 to Bagdad — A 20-mile drive to the north takes you through ruggedly beautiful high desert country to the small mining town of Bagdad. Named by William Lawler, supposedly a "diligent reader" of *Arabian Nights,* Bagdad never quite achieved the splendor of its namesake. While gold, bismuth, and tungsten mines all have operated in the area, it is the Cyprus Bagdad copper mine that has produced a fortune and is still working. Several large ranches also operate in the surrounding mountains.

142 Burro Creek Canyon — Named in 1869 by Army officers, the canyon (2 miles ahead) was probably populated by wild burros. Over time, Burro Creek has carved this canyon through basalt lava at the edge of the Aquarius Plateau. Looking downstream, one can see alternating layers of different colored lava. When it flows, Burro Creek runs into the Big Sandy River.

The entrance to Burro Creek Campground is just beyond this milepost. Situated in a ruggedly scenic area along the creek bed, the campground (modest fee) provides campsites, RV spaces, rest rooms, and water.

A scenic viewpoint is just southeast of the 964-foot single arch steel bridge that spans this canyon.

133 Signal — Near this milepost a dirt road leads southwest, crosses the Big Sandy several times, and in 15 miles meanders past the area of Signal. In 1877 this silver mining boom town came into being and within a year boasted a brewery and a peak population of 800. Ten years later the boom went bust, although the post office hung on until 1932. Today there is little to mark Signal's location except a few concrete slabs.

130 Big Sandy River — Beyond this milepost the highway descends into the broad, tree-lined valley of the Big Sandy River, so named because most of the time the river bed contains only sand and little or no water. Bluffs along both sides show a fantastic geologic history, a record of building up and cutting down. When running, the water meanders across the riverbed causing a braided channel. About 30 miles to the south, the Big Sandy and the Santa Maria join to form the Bill Williams River.

125 Wikieup — You are approaching the small roadside community of Wikieup, which offers restaurants, gas, and other services. The spring has made the area a popular encampment/settlement along the Big Sandy for centuries. One

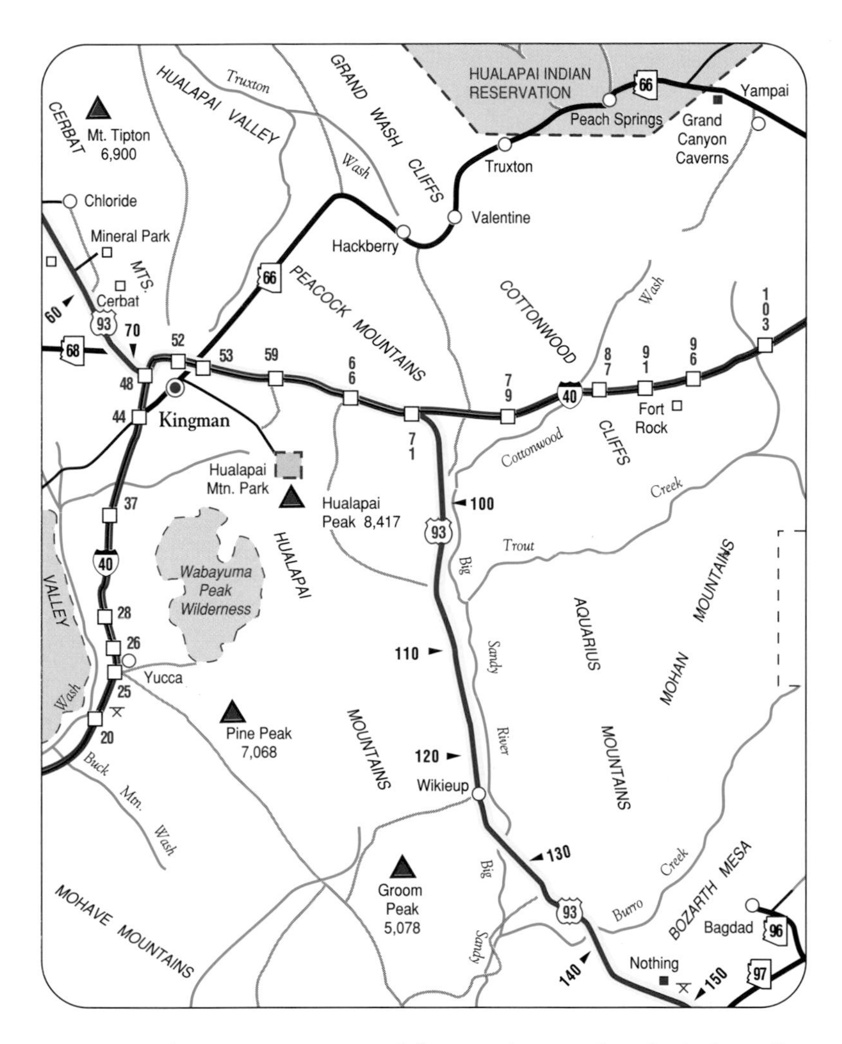

story says the town was named for a *wikieup,* a brush shelter of Apache origin, that stood near the spring when a name for the original post office was being considered in 1922.

122 Historical Marker — Just south of this milepost, on the east side of the highway, an historical marker provides a brief history of the Big Sandy Valley. It was occupied by various Indian tribes, explored by early Spaniards, and settled by ranchers and miners in the late 19th century. The rugged Aquarius Mountains, extending north and south, lie east of the valley and were named for the many small streams that run from them.

118-116 The Last Saguaros Going North — Near these mileposts, on hills to the west, are the last naturally growing saguaro cactus on your route north. Watch closely and see how many you can find in the next few miles.

101 **Hualapai Mountains** — West of the highway, angling in a northerly direction, are the Hualapai Mountains. Named for the Hualapai Indians of the area, they rise to a pine-clad summit of 8,417 feet. Situated about 30 minutes south of Kingman, these mountains are the setting for an exceptionally inviting Mohave County park and a number of summer cabins.

92 **Junction of U.S. 93 and Interstate 40** — Beyond this milepost, you will intersect Interstate 40 and turn west toward Kingman. (Note: The milepost sequencing changes to that of Interstate 40 and, beginning with Milepost 71, continues in descending order.)

70 **Juniper Trees** — Provided that soil and moisture conditions are right, juniper trees, with their dense, dark-green foliage, usually appear at altitudes above 3,500 feet. The elevation here is about 3,600 feet. For more information on junipers, see chapter 1, page 21, Milepost 276.

64 **Geography to the North** — Hualapai Valley is the broad plain running far to the north. The Cerbat Mountains rise to its west. The Cerbats mark another rich mineral area of the 19th century that played out decades ago. On the east side of the valley, far to the north, the outline of the steep Grand Wash Cliffs defines the southwest edge of the Colorado Plateau.

Exit 53 **Kingman and State Route 66** — Kingman once was an important way station on U.S. Route 66. Both the community and the highway were immortalized in an early TV series and the song "Route 66." The lyrics are still familiar to many: "Flagstaff, Arizona, don't forget Winona, Kingman, Barstow, San Bernardino...Get your kicks on Route 66." Still in use as State Route 66, the old road comes in from the northeast and intersects with Interstate 40 at this exit.

Exit 48 **Junction of Interstate 40 and U.S. 93** — To continue on to Lake Mead, exit at this point and head north on U.S. 93. Stops at Kingman's historic district and the Mohave Museum of History and Arts are recommended.

(Note: Once again milepost sequencing changes. Beginning with Milepost 71 it continues in descending order.)

70 Canotia Trees — The brushy trees on both sides of the road are *Canotia holocantha*. They resemble paloverde trees, but their bark is darker brown and they are found at higher elevations (2,500-4,500 feet). While these canotia are tree-size, some shrub-size versions in the same family carry the common names crown-of-thorns, crucifixion-thorn, and allthorn.

67 State Route 68 — Just before reaching this milepost, the highway to the west leads to the rapidly growing community of Bullhead City. The town was named for a rock formation in the Colorado River, which was covered by the waters of Lake Mohave when Davis Dam was completed. Across the Colorado is Laughlin, Nevada, a popular river-front resort and casino location.

61 Nearby Mountains and Abandoned Mines — The rugged mountains to the west are the Black Mountains. Running north-south and extending 100 miles tip-to-toe, they comprise one of the longest ranges in the state.

Directly to the east are the Cerbats (Coco-Maricopa Indian for bighorn sheep). The remains of many abandoned mines and ghost towns are located there, including the town of Cerbat, once the Mohave County seat. In this vicinity, on the east side of the highway, a historical marker provides a brief summary of the Cerbat's early mining days.

Proceeding north, one can't help but notice the long white line to the right. It's a huge tailings dump for the mine that ceased operation in 1981. However, ongoing recovery of copper continues by leaching the old dump. Behind the dump is Ithaca Peak. Once an imposing landmark, mining operations cut the

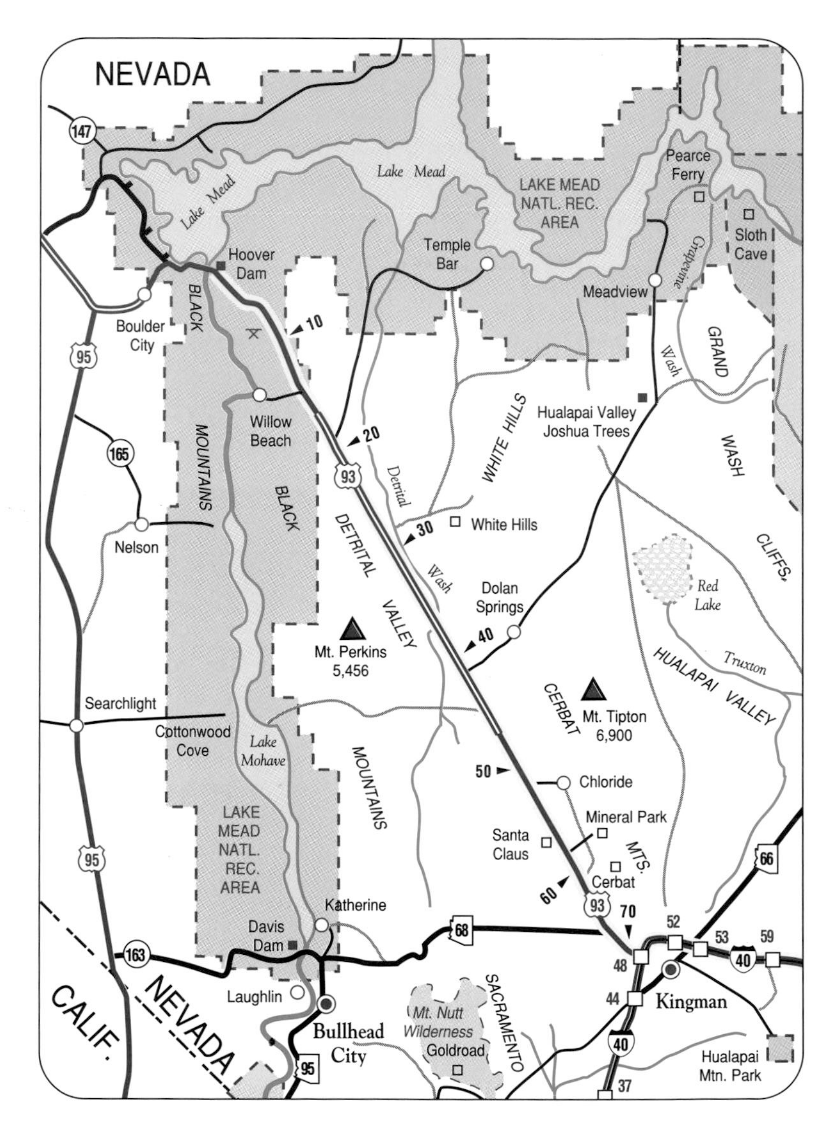

peak down to less than half its original height.

While today's scenery doesn't look anything like Mount St. Helens, these copper ores formed under that type of volcano 60 million years ago.

59 Mineral Park — Beyond this milepost a paved road leads to Mineral Park, 4 miles to the east. Visitors are not permitted on mine property, but you can still find a few scattered remains of the original community. Mineral Park too, for a brief time, was the Mohave County seat. Its name was selected because of the park-like setting between two mountains of minerals.

58 Santa Claus — Nearly half a century ago, an enterprising developer envisioned a Christmas-type community at this location, with architecture to match. Named Santa Claus, Arizona, the idea never went beyond what you now see on the west side of the highway.

53 Chloride — You are approaching the turnoff to Chloride, one of Arizona's oldest continuously inhabited mining communities. It was settled in 1864 as a silver-mining center. Some mining activity continues, but Chloride now features art shops, boutiques, restaurants, a tavern, and about 400 residents.

47 Divided Highway — As of this printing, U.S. Route 93 becomes a divided highway at this point. Plans call for the road to be improved all the way to Kingman.

42 Dolan Springs to Pearce Ferry — This paved road to the north takes you through the quiet communities of Dolan Springs and Meadview, then to the historic site of Pearce Ferry. If you like Joshua trees, the best stand in the world isn't at Joshua Tree National Monument, but just off this road (see map). In 1876 and the days before dams and bridges spanned the mighty Colorado, Pearce Ferry was a major crossing. It was the point where John Wesley Powell's expeditions stopped after their explorations of the Colorado River through the Grand Canyon. The last few miles of dirt road now lead only to a sandy beach.

36 Detrital Wash — "Detrital" is a rarely used adjective that means rocky debris. The old-timer who named Detrital Wash and Detrital Valley (running to the north and south) quite likely had an extensive vocabulary or a geology textbook.

29 White Hills — To the east 5 miles once thrived the mining town of White Hills. In May of 1892 an Indian named Hualapai Jeff was looking for iron oxide to use as face paint when he found silver ore instead. He showed the ore and its location to Judge Henry Shaffer who started the first mine in the area. Within two months, White Hills had 200 residents, a store, and saloons.

Two years later the population had grown beyond 1,500. The mine and town petered out by 1914. Today nothing remains.

20 Road to Temple Bar — Follow this paved road for 28 miles and you'll find Temple Bar, a vacation delight for those who enjoy quiet marinas. The fishing is great. Adventurous boaters can take a run up the lake into the Grand Canyon. The location offers lodging, a restaurant, boat and houseboat rentals, an RV park, and a tree-shaded campground. The name Temple Bar is derived from a gigantic rock formation in the middle of the lake that resembles a temple.

17 Lake Mead National Recreation Area — As the road narrows you enter the Lake Mead National Recreation Area. This region of convoluted formations was created by upthrusting layers of metamorphic rock and volcanic debris. The eroding force of the Colorado River has also contributed mightily to the wild look of the land.

15 Willow Beach Road — Just beyond this milepost a paved road runs 4.5 miles to Willow Beach on the Colorado River. The area offers a motel, RV park, restaurant, houseboat rental, and marina, but no camping is available in the narrow canyon. The location is known for its excellent fishing and trophy-sized trout. There is also Willow Beach National Fish Hatchery, which raises 850,000 trout per year. Tours of the facility are offered.

13 Scenic Overlook — On the west side of the highway (use caution when turning) a parking area and vista point provide an awesome view of the jade-green Colorado River at the bottom of its erosion-carved canyon. To the west across the river rise the rugged ridges of Nevada's Black Mountains.

9 Roadside Stop — Near this milepost you'll find a large roadside ramada and picnic tables.

6 Sand and Sediment — The wide areas of sand dunes and sediment through which you are now passing contrast with the rugged rock formations to the west of the river. As far back as 5 million years ago deep layers of sand and gravel covered the mountains of this region. Ages of wind and the force of the river have removed and shifted much of this material, exposing the earlier rock and volcanic formations. For rock hounds there are several good turnouts in the next few miles.

1 Hoover Dam and Lake Mead — A lookout point and parking area near this milepost provide a good view of the dam and Lake Mead. Additional parking areas near the dam are provided for those who want a closer look. Guided tours (modest fee) take a half-million visitors per year into the interior of the massive (3.2 million cubic yards of concrete), 726-foot-tall dam where 17 large turbines produce enough electricity to supply a city of a million people. The Alan Bible Visitor Center (named for the late Nevada senator) features exhibits and programs on Hoover Dam and the Lake Mead Recreational Area. It is located about 4 miles west near Boulder City, Nevada.

FOR YOUR TRAVELING CONVENIENCE READ EACH MILEPOST BEFORE YOU GET THERE.

Starting Point — This milepost trek begins in Flagstaff, a pine-clad north-central Arizona community located on Interstate 40. With a population of more than 40,000, Flagstaff (elevation 7,000 feet) is the home of Northern Arizona University, the Snowbowl ski area, and the Museum of Northern Arizona, which features one of the Southwest's finest collections of Native American art. Lowell Observatory, site of the 1930s discovery of the planet Pluto, is another well-known attraction.

Even before the town was established in the early 1880s, the area was a popular place to make camp because of several reliable sweetwater springs. The town got its name when immigrants in the area on July 4, 1876, raised an American flag on a tall pine. The "flagstaff" remained for years. Flagstaff, which grew up as a lumber, cattle, and railroad town, enjoys pleasant shirt-sleeve summers and, in winter months, occasional deep snow.

Along the Way — U.S. Route 89 stretches north for 137 miles to the Utah border. The serenity of long vistas and blue skies is part of the reward for this trip. Continuously changing views bombard the eye with geographical beauty.

The route also offers an introduction to Indian cultures that prize spiritual values, harmony with nature, and artistic endeavor. Shops, galleries, and trading posts feature Native American arts and crafts. The sparsely populated Navajo and Hopi reservations roll on to the east more than a hundred miles.

Outdoor activities run the gamut and include boating, fishing, and hiking. The mile-deep gorge of the Grand Canyon lies to the west of the highway. Near the end of your journey, Lake Powell's

(Left) The entrance to Sunset Crater Volcano National Monument is just north of Milepost 430.

160,000 acres of sapphire water stretch through canyons of massive red and buff sandstone cliffs.

On this tour mileposts are in ascending order.

MILEPOST HIGHLIGHTS

MILE 420

Mount Elden — To the west, as you proceed north from Interstate 40, is the impressive bulk of Mount Elden (elevation 9,299 feet), a volcanic center about 1 million years old. The southern slopes are nearly solid rock and feature columnar joints caused by shrinkage as the lava cooled. A forest fire in 1977 destroyed much of the mountain's timber on the eastern slope.

424 San Francisco Mountains — As you continue north, the bulk of the San Francisco Mountains to the west appear behind Mount Elden. Created by eruptions about 2.8 million years ago, these magnificent volcanic peaks, generally covered with snow from fall through late spring, offer some of the Southwest's finest skiing. The highest point in the range (and in Arizona) is Humphreys Peak at 12,643 feet. The summit was originally above 15,000 feet, but a sideward volcanic explosion and the effects of erosion have reduced the elevation.

The Hopi Indians believe their deities, the Kachinas, live in these mountains and hold the area as a sacred place.

425 Sunset Crater Volcano National Monument — Sunset Crater, named by Maj. John Wesley Powell for its colorful rim, is the large, reddish-black volcanic cone on the east side of the highway. Standing at about 2 o'clock, between black hills to the east and a forested peak to the west, this young cinder cone rises to 8,000 feet above sea level. The cone is composed of a half-billion tons of cinders formed as recently as the winter of A.D. 1064 - 1065. Because of its moon-like composition, NASA used this area as one of the sites to train the Apollo astronauts. The entrance to Sunset Crater Volcano National Monument is 5 miles ahead.

Twenty miles to the east, molten lava once flowed across the

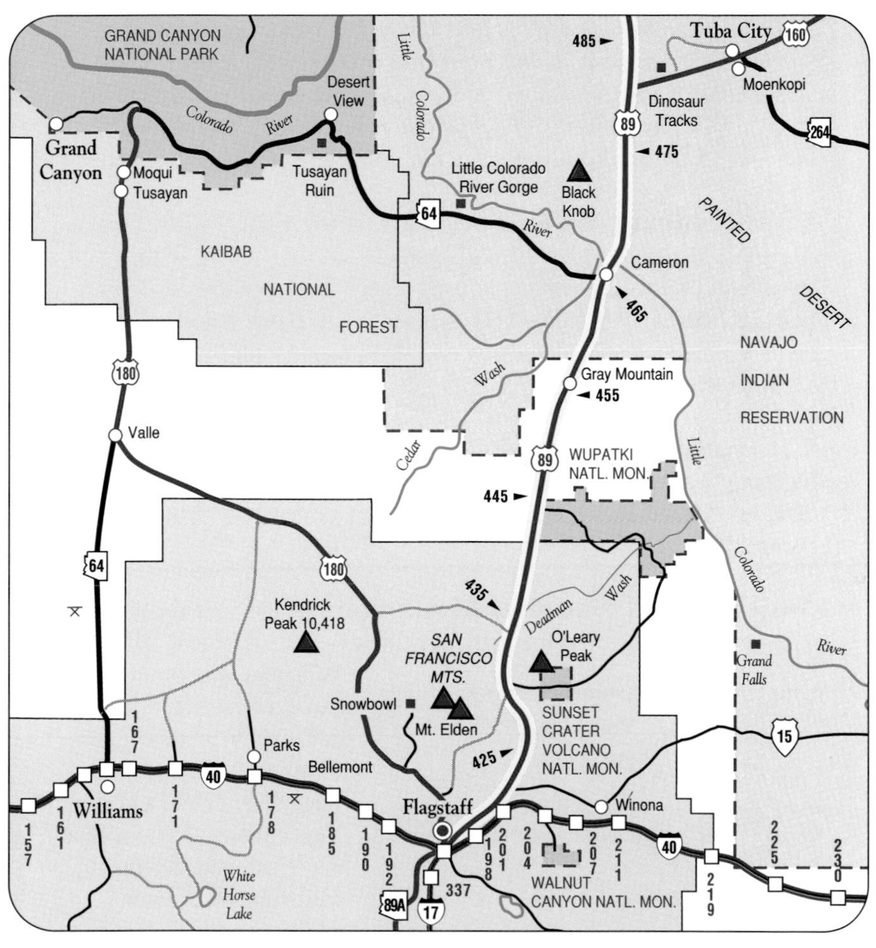

plateau and into the canyon of the Little Colorado River, forming a gigantic dam. The region behind the dam has long since filled with silt. Now, when the intermittent Little Colorado runs around the lava flow and cascades back into its original canyon, the resulting Grand Falls are higher than Niagara's.

431 Ponderosa Pine Forest — At this milepost a deep forest of ponderosa pine surrounds you. An uninterrupted stretch of this high-country timber continues east and south through the White Mountains and into New Mexico. Lumbering has been an important industry in this area since the late 1800s. Only a few miles ahead, the elevation drops, giving way to rolling grassland dotted with juniper and piñon pine.

433 O'Leary Peak — Directly to the east is 8,916-foot O'Leary Peak. Unlike barren Sunset Crater, this volcanic peak supports a growth of timber and has a road to its crest (Forest Route 545A, which is located about a quarter-mile west of the Sunset Crater Visitor Center). Passenger cars must park at the gate, a mile from the top. High-clearance vehicles can drive all the way to the lookout tower at the summit if the gate is open.

434 Deadman Wash and Deadman Flat — Just before reaching Milepost 435, you will cross Deadman Wash, with Deadman Flat to the east. Some tales say that cowboys driving a herd of horses were killed in this area by Indians. Another story deals with the murder of a traveler. Yet another cites a suicide. You decide.

435 Flagstaff Volcanic Field — As you drive along the highway, the extent of volcanic activity in this area is not obvious. However, more than 400 cinder cones have been counted in this region.

444 Wupatki National Monument — To visit these extensive prehistoric ruins, turn east just before Milepost 445. Wupatki was built after Sunset Crater erupted in A.D. 1064 or 1065. Strangely, the volcano had a beneficial effect. The cinders that covered the earth soaked up moisture from later rainstorms and retarded evaporation. The natives of the area soon discovered this natural mulch and their crops flourished for generations.

At Wupatki you can explore ruins of structures built by the prehistoric ancestors of today's Hopi Indians — large multistoried pueblos, a precisely engineered outdoor amphitheater, a large ball court, and other structures.

Wupatki can also be reached by a loop road from Sunset Crater. A single fee permits you to visit both monuments (see text on Milepost 425).

457 Gray Mountain Trading Post — Named for the gray-colored mountains to the northwest, the area is more than just a trading post. Gray Mountain offers two motels (one with a swimming pool), a restaurant, groceries, and gas. And Indian arts and crafts, of course.

458 Navajo Indian Reservation — You have just entered the largest Indian Reservation in the United States. As you proceed north, you will travel only the western edge of this 25,000-square-mile expanse of starkly beautiful country. The reservation extends into New Mexico and Utah and is home to nearly 75,000 Navajos. The nation's capital is Window Rock, 135 miles east as the crow flies.

465 State Route 64 to Grand Canyon — Fifty-one miles to the west, the Grand Canyon's Desert View Overlook provides a memorable view into the canyon's erosion-blasted depths. Grand Canyon Village is an additional 25 miles west on Route 64. Entrance fee.

466 Cameron — One of the Southwest's truly historic trading posts, Cameron was established in 1911 by Hubert Richardson when the single-lane steel bridge was completed. The bridge (now closed) once provided the region's only automobile crossing of the Little Colorado River. The post was named after U.S. Sen. Ralph H. Cameron and today offers a wide selection of jewelry, rugs, baskets, and pottery from the Navajo, Hopi, and New Mexico Pueblo Indians. Don't miss the Indian art gallery and the old hotel on the banks of the river gorge.

469 Navajo Roadside Vendors — The stands on the west side of the highway are typical of those found along major roads all over the reservation. All are operated by Navajo merchants who take great pride in their handcrafted products.

473 Painted Desert and Black Knob — The barren, multicolored Painted Desert stretches to the east and southeast for more than a hundred miles. Ancient deposits of minerals in the geologic layers of the Chinle formation tint the sands with shades of blue-gray, faded plum, soft vermilion, and other colors. The colors glow vividly in early morning and late afternoon light. To the west is Black Knob. Called Shadow Mountain by locals and on some maps, it is a small volcanic cone that stands above the surrounding land.

476 Navajo Hogans — About a half-mile north of this milepost several traditional Navajo hogans (houses) seem to grow from the land on the west side of the highway. They have a crib-log design, usually constructed with eight sides and a door facing east. Beyond Milepost 477, on the east side of the highway, an updated version of a hogan maintains the octagonal design but is constructed of modern materials.

480 Junction of U.S. Route 160 — Just before reaching Milepost 481, U.S. Highway 160 angles to the east. Three miles down this highway you can view ancient dinosaur tracks left in the mud millions of years ago when this area was a marshy lowland. Another 7 miles takes you to Tuba City. Named for a Hopi leader, it is one of the reservation's largest towns (population 5,000). Southeast of Tuba City about 50 miles on State Route 264, the Hopi mesas and the village of Oraibi, the oldest continuously inhabited community in the United States, rise from the surrounding desert.

486 Beginning of Echo Cliffs — The red sandstone cliffs to the east will continue to rise for the next 50 miles until they attain vertical heights of more than 1,000 feet. Named by Maj. John Wesley Powell when they echoed gunshots during his first exploration of the Colorado River, these up-tilted Jurassic sandstone slabs were created by deposits laid down in the ocean bottom more than 138 million years ago. Note the small oasis about a mile north; it is caused by a spring seeping out of the rocks high on the cliffs.

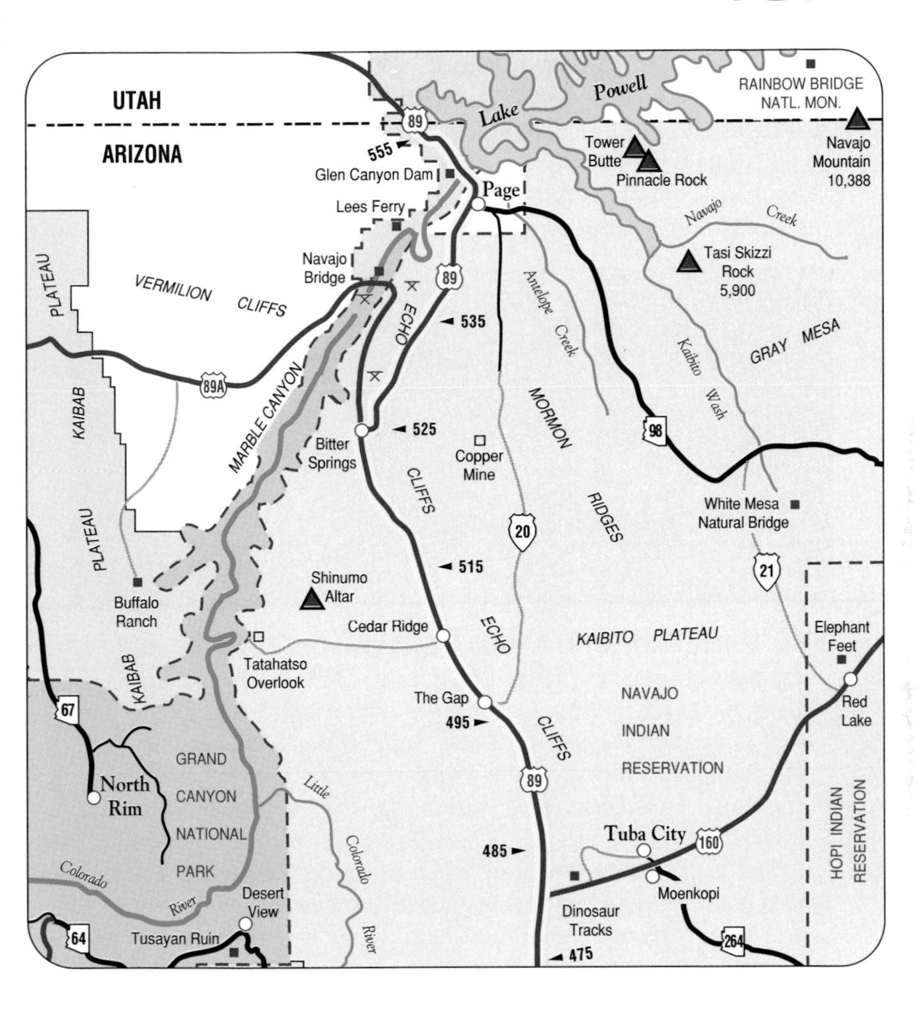

Arizona Historical Society

493 Hamblin Wash — The usually dry stream bed between the highway and Echo Cliffs is named after Jacob Hamblin, the Mormon missionary and explorer who trailblazed in northern Arizona more than a century ago. Hamblin was also the architect of a peace treaty between early settlers and the Navajo Indians. After rare rainstorms the wash can turn into a raging torrent.

498 The Gap — An elementary school and a few homes are found here. This is the only natural gap in the cliffs for more than 50 miles.

505 Cedar Ridge — Just north of the sign for the small settlement of Cedar Ridge, a dirt road heads west. If you are driving a high-clearance vehicle, this poor road winds 21 miles to remote Tatahatso Overlook on the upper Grand Canyon. The view is inspiring, but be advised that there are confusing forks in the road and no services.

520 Vermilion Cliffs and Honeymoon Trail — To the north are the soaring escarpments of the 2,000-foot Vermilion Cliffs that run east and west for more than a hundred miles.

A 19th century wagon road, the Honeymoon Trail, once ran south from Utah, followed the Vermilion Cliffs east, crossed the Colorado River at Lees Ferry, and then turned south along the Echo Cliffs. You are now on a section of highway that generally follows the old route. Its name came from the Mormon couples who traveled this arduous trail in covered wagons from central and eastern Arizona to seal their marriage vows at the temple in St. George, Utah.

523 Bitter Springs — Named for the bitter taste of the waters from the springs, this small community of homes indicates that some Navajo like the conveniences of modern living. Many, however, still adhere to the traditional way of life and prefer to live in hogans in more remote areas.

524 Junction of U.S. 89 and U.S. 89A — Route 89 turns east at this point, going up and over the Echo Cliffs to Page, Glen Canyon Dam, and Lake Powell. Route 89A, branching to the north and west, leads to one of the most isolated regions in the U.S., the Arizona Strip. This 9,000-square-mile area has fewer than 5,000 people. Scenic highlights accessed by this route include Marble Canyon, historic Lees Ferry across the Colorado, the North Rim of the Grand Canyon, and the historic Mormon fort at Pipe Spring National Monument.

527 Scenic Pullout on the Echo Cliffs — For a spectacular view, stop in the parking area on the west side of the highway. The dark blue bulk on the western horizon is the Kaibab Plateau. *Kaibab* is a Paiute word for "mountain lying down." At 2 o'clock you'll see the sweep of the Vermilion Cliffs. The meandering scar on the flatlands below is Marble Canyon, nearly 500 feet deep, with the Colorado River at its bottom.

Beyond Milepost 527 the road passes through a giant cut in the cliffs. This enormous task was completed in 1957 as a necessary precondition for the hauling of the thousands of truckloads of concrete used in the construction of Glen Canyon Dam.

530 Navajo Mountain — The distant crest of Navajo Mountain rises beyond the eastern horizon at a 2 o'clock position. More of this soaring 10,388-foot peak will soon come into view. One of the four sacred mountains of the Navajo Indians, it is part of the exceedingly rugged country in the vicinity of Glen Canyon and the twisting gorge of the San Juan River.

542 Wind and Water Erosion — Just before Milepost 542 are fine examples of sandstone that has been eroded by the wind into unusual shapes. At the milepost the highway crosses Water Holes Canyon. You can stop to peer down into this "slot" canyon. It is typical of the water erosion in the area.

547 Business Loop to Page — The town of Page, named for John Chatfield Page, a U.S. Bureau of Reclamation commissioner, grew out of the sand and sagebrush when construction of Glen Canyon Dam began in 1957. The community of about 8,000 provides services for visitors who come to view the magnificent scenery and to enjoy the fishing, boating, and water sports opportunities offered by nearby Lake Powell.

If time permits, visit the John Wesley Powell Museum dedicated to the memory of the explorer and scientist who, in 1869, led the first boat expedition down the Colorado River. Exhibits feature historic photographs, mineral and fossil displays, Indian artifacts, and pioneer memorabilia.

548 Scenic Overlook, Colorado River — Just north of Milepost 548, an unpaved road leads to an excellent view of the 710-foot face of Glen Canyon Dam with the canyon's steel bridge in the foreground and Lake Powell beyond. A trail leads to a vista point that looks down on the Colorado River.

549 Glen Canyon Dam, Lake Powell — Here you cross Glen Canyon, with the dam and Lake Powell to the north, and the Colorado River running south. The Carl Hayden Visitor Center, named for the long-time U.S. senator from Arizona, offers exhibits and information on the construction of the dam and the geologic history of the area. Free, self-guided tours into the interior of the dam are also offered.

550 Entrance to Wahweap Marina and Lodge — The turnoff takes you to the shoreline of Lake Powell where a large marina and the accommodations of Wahweap Lodge draw visitors from all over the world. The lake extends 186 miles and, counting all the side canyons, has more than 1,900 miles of shoreline. Half-day and full-day boat excursions on Lake Powell are offered.

552 Scenic Overlook, Lake Powell — Just north of Milepost 552, an unpaved road to the east ascends a small hill, providing a panoramic view of Lake Powell. In its main channel the lake plunges to depths of more than 500 feet. Submerged along its course are numerous ancient Indian ruins scuba divers sometimes explore.

557 Leave Arizona, Enter Utah 

TOUR PHOTOGRAPHS BY DAVID ELMS, JR.

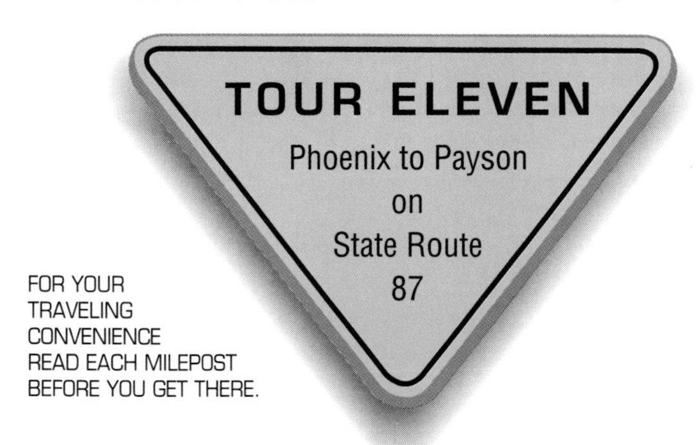

FOR YOUR TRAVELING CONVENIENCE READ EACH MILEPOST BEFORE YOU GET THERE.

Starting Point — Your tour starts in Phoenix, the state capital of Arizona. For a brief profile of Phoenix, turn to page 27.

Along the Way — Milepost markers for this 74-mile trip begin north of Mesa and head toward the high country below the towering Mogollon Rim. You will cross two Indian reservations, be treated to panoramic views of the Superstition Mountains, and travel through lush areas of the lower Sonoran Desert.

Dirt side roads afford opportunities for hiking and exploring by auto. You will see a strangely sculpted wonderland of rocks, negotiate deep canyons of the Mazatzal Mountains, and end your trip in the attractive, mile-high community of Payson. Mileposts are in ascending order.

MILEPOST HIGHLIGHTS

The Beeline Highway — Milepost 178 on State Route 87 north of Mesa is near the McDowell Road intersection. This north-south route is known locally as the Beeline Highway, because it offers the only "beeline" route through some of Arizona's most rugged country. Completed in 1959, the present highway opened the vast high country around the Mogollon Rim to hikers, campers, and summer vacationers. The earliest road through this difficult region was an 1860s wagon trail extending east along Sycamore Creek from Fort McDowell to Sunflower, through a mountain pass to Camp Reno in the Tonto Basin, then north to Payson.

(Left) Near Milepost 226 State Route 87 winds through the Mazatzal Mountains and descends Slate Creek Hill enroute to Payson.

179 Salt River Indian Reservation — For the next 13 miles you will be crossing land that belongs to the Pima and Maricopa Indians. Established in 1879, the reservation covers nearly 50,000 acres. Along State Route 87 the land is largely undeveloped, but to the west, thousands of acres are under irrigated cultivation. One of the Valley's largest shopping malls, a junior college, and a new residential area are also situated on tribal land.

180 Superstition and McDowell Mountains — To the east of the highway several mountain ranges appear to interlock. Most southerly (at a 2 o'clock position) are the Superstition Mountains. This great, looming mass with nearly sheer cliffs was born in a frenzy of volcanic activity more than 15 million years ago. The Superstitions are the alleged site of the legendary Lost Dutchman gold mine.

The ragged desert peaks, standing at a 10 o'clock position northwest of the highway, are the McDowell Mountains.

181 Creosote Bushes — In this area you will see an abundance of dull-green, low-growing creosote bushes on both sides of the highway. Some botanists believe these are the oldest living things on earth. Some specimens have been judged to be nearly 12,000 years of age. A central plant sends out runners that pop up as extensions of the original. What appears to be numerous creosote bushes may be only one plant. This process of expansion continues for centuries.

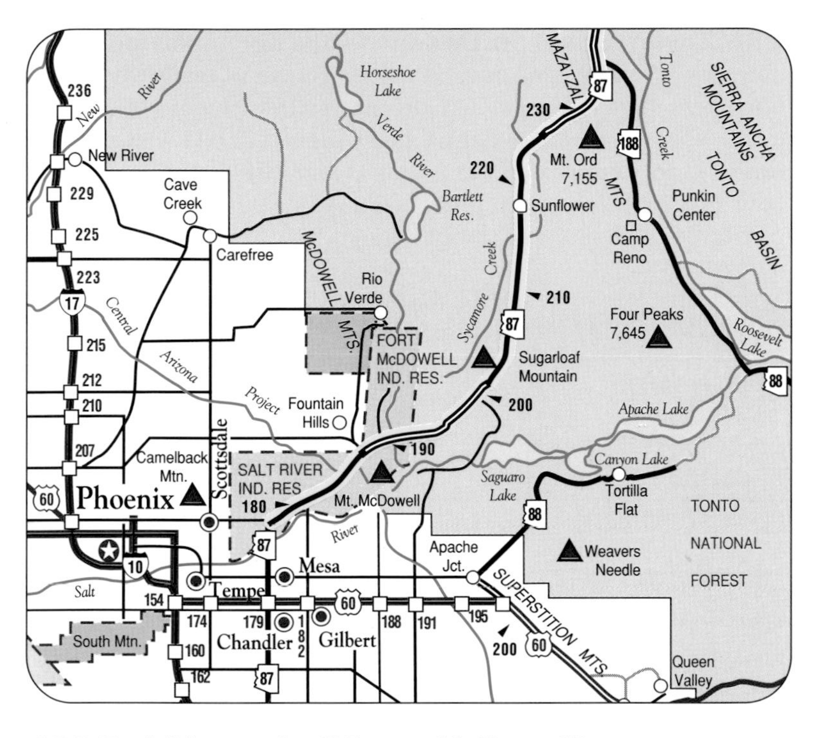

182 Red Mountain (Mount McDowell) — On maps the strangely shaped, reddish peak straight ahead is listed as Mount McDowell or McDowell Peak, but locally it is called Red Mountain. The McDowell mountains, Mount McDowell, and nearby Fort McDowell were named for Gen. Irvin McDowell, commander of U.S. troops in California and Arizona, circa 1865. During turbulent frontier days, the peak was used as a lookout point to scan the horizon for Apache war parties. The mountain is also said to have been a sacred area to the ancient Hohokam people who inhabited this region nearly 2,000 years ago.

184 The Arizona Canal — Beyond this milepost you will cross the Arizona Canal, one of the primary water lifelines for the greater Phoenix area. The canal has been in use since 1887, when water was diverted by a brush dam below the confluence of the Salt and Verde rivers. Since then, Granite Reef Dam, Stewart Mountain Dam, Roosevelt Dam, and several other modern dams have been built along the course of the Salt River.

186 Lower Sonoran Desert — The land in this area, at an elevation of about 1,300 feet, is representative of the lower Sonoran geographic zone. Dominant growth includes tall saguaro cactus with their upraised arms, many-jointed cholla with needle-sharp spines, and rotund barrel cactus with fishhook-like spines. Low growing trees are mesquite, with dark, rough bark, and paloverde, with limbs of smooth, green bark.

187 Central Arizona Project Aqueduct — Just ahead is another man-made waterway. This one starts at the Colorado River on the state's western border and runs 330 miles to a point south of Tucson. The aqueduct carries nearly 2 billion gallons of water per day to farms and communities along its route.

188 Fountain Hills and McDowell Mountain Park — A left turn at the traffic light at Shea Boulevard will take you to the community of Fountain Hills where more than 10,000 people reside. Fountain Hills features the world's highest fountain. During 15-minute periods from 10 A.M. until 9 P.M., the fountain shoots water 560 feet into the desert air.

McDowell Mountain Regional Park, accessed by going north 7 miles on Fountain Hills Boulevard, offers campgrounds (some with hookups, modest fee), picnic areas, hiking and equestrian trails, and a shooting range in a magnificent desert setting.

189 Fort McDowell Indian Reservation — Just before reaching this milepost you enter the Fort McDowell Indian Reservation. The fort was established by Gen. Irvine McDowell in 1865 and abandoned in 1890. In 1891, the 25,000 acres were turned over to members of the Yavapai tribe.

190 Fort McDowell Recreation Area — At the intersection beyond this milepost you can turn south to an unusual wildlife park inhabited by big cats from Asia, Africa, and North America (there is a fee).

The road north goes to the Fort McDowell Gaming Center. Open seven days a week, the large facility offers high-stakes bingo and electronic casino games. The road north also leads to a picnic and recreation area near the banks of the Verde River.

At the northwest corner of the intersection stand three historical markers. One mentions the unlikely career of Wassaja, a Mojave-Apache child who was captured by Pima Indians in 1871 and sold to a white settler. Wassaja, thereafter known as Carlos Montezuma, graduated *cum laude* from the University of Illinois and became a noted physician in Chicago for many years. He was a strong spokesman for Indian rights, and later returned to the reservation. He is buried in a marked grave a few miles north of the intersection.

191 Verde River — With headwaters located about 20 miles north of Prescott in north-central Arizona, the Verde (Spanish for "green") is a major contributor to the water needs of central Arizona. A couple of miles downstream it joins the Salt River above Granite Reef Dam and is diverted into canals that serve a 3,000-square-mile area in and around metropolitan Phoenix.

193 Tonto National Forest — Beyond this milepost you will pass an entrance sign to Tonto National Forest. While the land here contains desert vegetation, this dedicated area stretches across nearly 3 million acres and includes extensive pine forests and peaks approaching 8,000 feet.

199 Turnoff to Saguaro Lake — About 2 miles to the south, off the Bush Highway, 10-mile-long Saguaro Lake nestles into the desert canyon of the Salt River. The lake offers boating

and boat rentals, a restaurant, fishing, and camping. A mile farther south is the Lower Salt River Recreation Area, perhaps the inner-tubing capital of the world. On busy weekends (May through September) thousands of people rent inner tubes and float the Salt River's 8-mile stretch between Stewart Mountain Dam and Granite Reef Dam. Shuttles return floaters to the starting point and have five pickup stops along the route. There is a fee for a tube and the shuttle pass.

202 **Desert Vista** — This stop features a paved parking lot, a ramada for shade, and a short botanical hike along a man-made path. Various desert plants are identified and described. The area also offers an excellent view of Four Peaks in the Mazatzal Mountains directly to the east. To the southeast you can see the immense, upthrusting spire of Weaver's Needle in the Superstition Mountains. The tall, thumb-shaped pinnacle (1,300 feet from base to top) supposedly casts a shadow across the shaft of the legendary Lost Dutchman mine. However, gold-seekers have been following the shadow for more than a century without locating the mine.

203 **Sugarloaf Mountain** — Just beyond this milepost a dirt road to the north provides a trip to Sugarloaf Mountain and usually dry Sycamore Creek. Flat-topped Sugarloaf is just one of 13 peaks in Arizona bearing that name. In 1867, the U.S. Cavalry trail from Fort McDowell to Payson (then called Green Valley) followed along the banks of Sycamore Creek for over 20 miles.

204 Wonderland of Rocks — The foothills just ahead provide graphic evidence of the long-term power of wind, rain, and blowing sand. About 1.4 billion years ago a mass of granite was forced upward in this region by a great wrenching of the earth's upper plates. The mass cracked like a shattering windshield. Across the centuries erosion has worked at the cracks, slowly but inexorably shaping the pieces into the intriguing formations on both sides of the highway.

205 Saguaro Cactus — The hills and canyons in this area are covered with tall saguaro cactus that grow only in the lower Sonoran Desert. With increases in elevation, they will disappear beyond Milepost 230. The tallest living saguaro is located in a remote desert area about 60 miles southwest of Phoenix, where it stands 57 feet, 11 inches tall. Test your brakes at this milepost. There is a steep downhill stretch ahead.

206 Old Bush Highway — To the right, at the bottom of the valley, you can see a small portion of the original road that ran between Phoenix and Payson. "Washboard" describes its condition in those days, as do hot, dusty, and tiring. The meandering trip — assuming the creek crossings were dry, you didn't stop too long for a picnic lunch, and didn't have any flat tires or mechanical problems — took five hours or more.

212 Sycamore Creek, Screwtail Hill — Hard rain can turn Sycamore into a raging torrent. In 1970 a sudden deluge sent an immense wall of water down the creek. It washed away the embankments at either end of the bridge, but left the asphalt deceptively in place. A Highway Patrol car was the first vehicle to approach the bridge. It plunged through the unsupported strip of pavement and the officer was swept away.

The old wagon road crossed Sycamore not far upstream from here. For the next 5 miles its usual condition was *very rough* and *very steep*. Seemingly countless switchbacks earned it the name Screwtail Hill. As one old-timer who frequently made the dusty trip said, "If they'd only pave this (bleep) road I'd never complain about anything else again."

218 Sunflower and Mount Ord — In 1868 Sunflower served as a cavalry watering station. Known as Camp O'Connell, it was a temporary site while building the old military road from Fort McDowell to Camp Reno and on to Payson. The Army abandoned Camp Reno in April, 1870. The Apaches were surprised to find it empty and burned it to the ground.

The high point on Mount Ord, directly ahead, is Eagle Peak at 7,153 feet. The mountain is named for Gen. Edward O.C. Ord, Commander of the Department of California in the late 1860s.

225 Changing Geographical Zone — Note that the hillsides now exhibit bushy, low-growing juniper trees, piñon pine, and oak trees. At an altitude of 4,300 feet, you are moving out of the lower Sonoran zone into the upper Sonoran zone. Notice, too, that the saguaros have disappeared. The downhill incline just ahead will take you back to an altitude of about 3,300 feet where the giant cactus will make a final appearance.

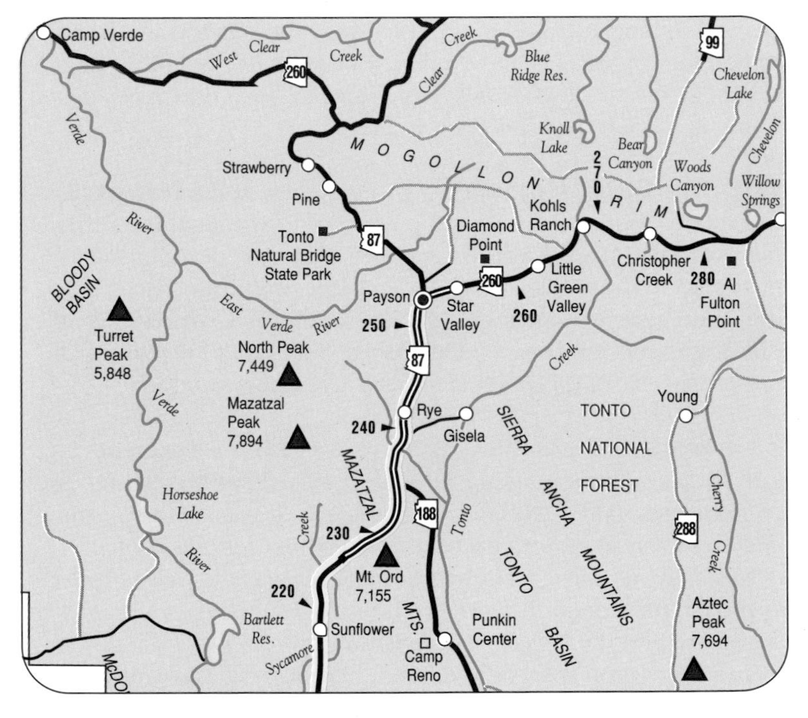

226 Slate Creek Hill — This downhill stretch of highway into Slate Creek Canyon was a treacherous road in the days before it was paved. The slate made for an alternately slippery and tire-chewing surface. If you examine the mountainsides closely, patches of the old road still can be seen. At the bottom of the hill the Ord Mine once extracted mercury from the mountain.

229 The Last Saguaro — Just before reaching Milepost 230, look beyond the highway embankment on the left side of the highway. The small maverick saguaro growing in the rocky soil is the last to be seen as you proceed north to Payson.

Wesley Holden

232 Tonto Basin — You are now descending the eastern foothills of the Mazatzal Mountains. To the east are the rugged lowlands of the Tonto Basin. Translated from Spanish, the word *tonto* means "stupid" or "crazy." The peaceful White Mountain Apaches bestowed this derisive nickname on a fierce group of related Indians (the Tonto Apaches) because they refused to make peace with the whites. Arizona place names now include Tonto National Forest, Tonto Mountain, Tonto Village and Tonto Fish Hatchery, to mention only a few.

235 State Route 188 — Beyond this milepost a paved highway angles southeast for 33 miles to Theodore Roosevelt Dam and the 17,000-acre lake behind it. The area offers excellent fishing, a marina, campgrounds, a trailer park, a motel, and groceries. Tonto National Monument, 5 miles east of the dam, houses cliff dwellings of the ancient Salado culture.

236 Eastern Slopes of the Mazatzal Mts. — The highest point directly to the west is Mazatzal Peak at 7,903 feet above sea level. The most northerly peak is North Peak, which is 7,449 feet in elevation. The name

Mazatzal, translated from the Apache, means "bleak or barren." It is pronounced locally as "mat-a-zel."

Part of these mountains are set aside as the Mazatzal Wilderness. One of the state's most rugged areas, it rises from sun-baked desert to high, cool pines. Wildlife in the wilderness ranges from rattlesnakes to black bears, and jack rabbits to mountain lions.

239 Gisela and Rye — Beyond this milepost, at the north end of the bridge, a paved road winds through the hills and canyons for 5 miles to the town of Gisela. Located on the banks of Tonto Creek at the base of the towering Sierra Ancha Mountains, the community was originally established in 1894 and named by an early-day schoolteacher who happened to be

Richard Maack

reading a novel titled *Countess Gisela* (locally pronounced guy-*see*-la). However it is pronounced, Gisela is a popular spot for people who like to live off the beaten path. Gisela has a tavern, a store, and a small cafe.

The settlement of Rye, on State Route 87 just beyond the turnoff to Gisela, boasts what may be the largest used motorcycle and bicycle collection in the universe. This was originally the ranch of Sam Haught. Early settlers named Rye Creek for the luxuriant growth of wild rye they found here. The post office was closed in 1907.

241 Oxbow Hill — Two explanations for the name come from *Arizona Place Names*. One is that ox yokes were found on the mountain by early settlers in pursuit of Indians who had stolen some livestock. The other is that the old road made two perfect loops up the mountain resembling an oxbow (which, in fact, it did). The long hill has seen many boiling car radiators. Additional heat comes from the tempers of drivers waiting to pass slow vehicles. This was the first stretch of State Route 87 to be divided.

250 Mogollon Rim — Directly ahead you can see the nearly sheer escarpments of the Mogollon Rim, a natural dividing line between Arizona's central highlands and the vast northern sweep of the Colorado Plateau. The Rim, named for Spanish governor Don Juan Ignacio Flores de Mogollon, Captain General of New Mexico from 1712-15, extends more than 300 miles across Arizona and into New Mexico. The Rim often presents cliffs nearly 2,000 feet high.

In 1990 a lightning strike caused Arizona's most destructive forest fire, destroying nearly 25,000 acres of timber and claiming the lives of six firefighters. The damage of the Dude fire cannot be seen from State Route 87 south of Payson. Check with the Ranger Station on State Route 260 just east of Payson for a self-guided tour brochure and directions to the burn area.

251 Entering Payson — Historically, Payson was a ranching and logging center. Today it is also a haven for people who like an unhurried lifestyle, an abundance of outdoor activities, and fresh mountain air. At an elevation of almost 5,000 feet, Payson offers four distinct seasons with light winter snows and cool summer days. Its population is approaching 10,000 permanent residents. The community offers a full range of services for visitors, including motels, restaurants, auto service, and retail stores. If you plan to continue your journey through Arizona's high country, a milepost tour from Payson to Show Low on State Route 260 appears on page 155.

TOUR PHOTOGRAPHS BY DAVID ELMS, JR.

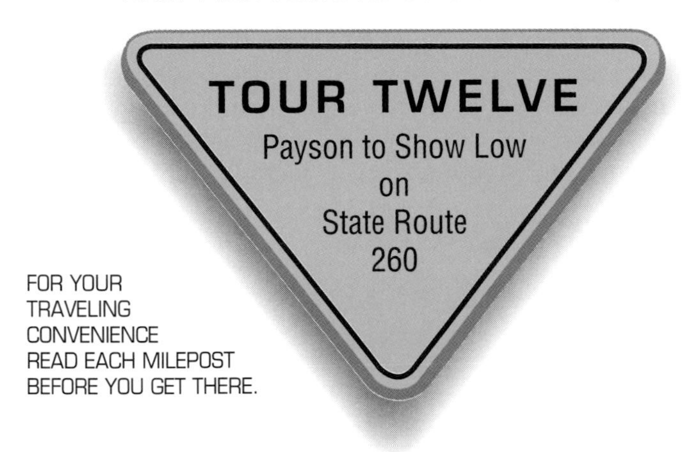

FOR YOUR TRAVELING CONVENIENCE READ EACH MILEPOST BEFORE YOU GET THERE.

Starting Point — Payson, a mile-high, pine-country community, started out as a ranching and lumbering center. Today, however, Payson is best known as a town that serves a growing tourist trade. During summer months, the lure of its cool, mountain climate swells Payson's permanent population of about 10,000 to more than 30,000 on busy weekends.

The town offers a wide range of lodging, numerous restaurants, and retail stores. However, during peak periods, it's a good idea to make overnight reservations in advance. All-season, outdoor recreational opportunities are almost limitless.

For more information, visit the Payson Chamber of Commerce at the corner of Main Street and State Route 87.

Along the Way — This trip takes you east through what is popularly known as "Zane Grey Country," thousands of square miles of thickly forested mountains and canyons where the novelist lived and worked while creating many of his Western epics. The most inspiring geography is provided by the soaring 2,000-foot escarpment of the colorful Mogollon Rim.

This impressive drop-off point between the vast Colorado Plateau and Arizona's central highlands is a rich repository of early history. Famed frontier general George Crook built one of the West's most famous trails along the Mogollon Rim — a bumpy, wagon route that stretched from Prescott's Fort Whipple to Fort Apache in the White Mountain country to the southeast.

Along the way, you will climb to elevations approaching 8,000 feet, cross babbling trout streams, pass through lush meadows where elk sometimes graze, and encounter numerous side roads

(Left) Along the east bank of Tonto Creek, near Milepost 269, a Forest Service road winds north past the site where Zane Grey's cabin once stood.

that lead to remote and awe-inspiring regions. Your tour will end in Show Low, a gateway community to Arizona's breathtaking White Mountain region. (For an account of frontier travel along this trail read *Vanished Arizona* by Martha Summerhayes.)

Mileposts along the 90-mile trip are in ascending order.

MILEPOST HIGHLIGHTS

Junction, State Routes 87 and 260 — Your tour starts near the business center of Payson, then heads east toward Show Low over a modern highway. At one time this region was one of the more isolated in Arizona. In the early 1900s, Payson was connected to the outside world only by a pair of primitive dirt roads, one running north to Flagstaff, the other south to Globe.

MILE 252

Payson Ranger Station — Nearly to Milepost 253, turn south to the U.S. Forest Service ranger station. Here you'll find information on hiking, natural history, and attractions in the region. If you are interested in viewing the devastation caused by the 1990 Dude fire that destroyed nearly 25,000 acres of timberland along the Mogollon Rim, the ranger station has a self-guided tour brochure that will take you through the area. If you want only a quick glance at the fire zone, forego the self-guided tour and follow our directions from Milepost 267.

255 **Star Valley** — This small community is growing as the result of rapid increases in the local vacation trade. It is named after John Starr, who settled in this area in the late 1870s. The site offers accommodations and retail services for Rim country visitors.

257 **Diamond Point** — To the north looms scenic Diamond Point named for its "Arizona diamonds," quartz crystals that are occasionally found throughout the region. A road to the north leads to the appropriately named residential area of Diamond Point Shadows. To drive to the fire lookout atop Diamond Point, continue east on State Route 260 to Milepost 267, then take Forest Road 64.

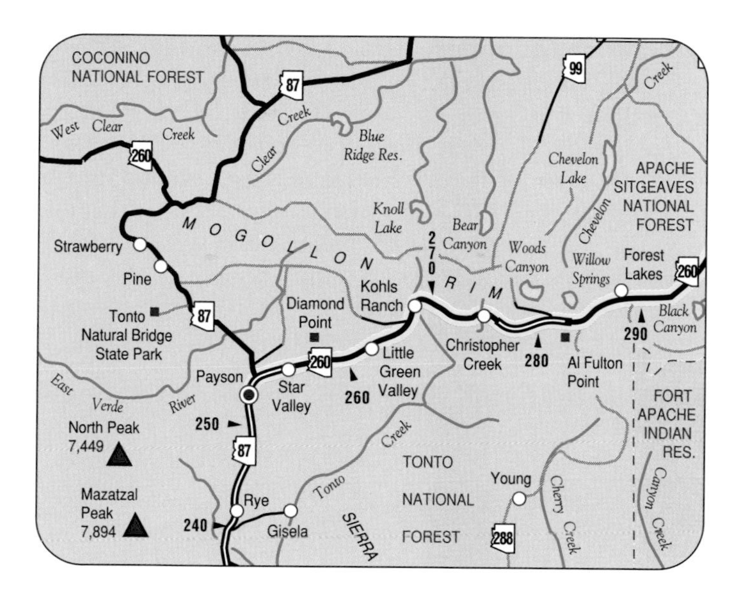

258 Payson Zoo — Beyond this milepost, just south of the highway on Lion Springs Road, this private home for exotic and indigenous animals — many trained for motion picture performances — is a treat for children and adults alike.

The animals, conditioned for close human contact, relate more directly with visitors than do animals in larger zoos. Included are leopards, baboons, and tigers, as well as many North American species. There is a fee.

261 Preacher Canyon — In the 1880s, when the Pleasant Valley War (a feud between frontier families) was raging in this region, a preacher lived in the canyon just ahead. Being a neutral party, the cleric (to identify himself) sang gospel songs in a loud voice as he wandered his missionary way through the deep forests. It is said that as an added precaution he also carried a loaded double-barreled shotgun. Folks who sought to immortalize his courage could not, unfortunately, recall his name. Thus, Preacher Canyon.

263 Little Green Valley — Deer and elk frequently graze in this lush mountain meadow surrounded by thick timber. Corrals and houses indicate that the people living here have also found the location appealing. The Payson area was originally known as Green Valley, hence the qualifier "little" for this lovely place.

Forest Road 405A leads east from here to the Hells Gate Wilderness, a beautiful but rugged canyon protected as a designated wilderness area by the U.S. Forest Service.

264 View of Mogollon Rim — As you approach Milepost 265, you will see an exceptional view of the soaring cliffs of the Mogollon Rim. It is believed that the name is derived from that of Don Juan Ignacio Flores de Mogollon, governor of New Mexico (1712-15). The Rim, which extends across Arizona and into New Mexico for more than 300 miles, was formed by up-lifting and erosion that began more than 25 million years ago — that's long before the mighty Colorado River started sculpting the Grand Canyon. The line of cliffs, sometimes 2,000 feet high, forms the southern lip of the vast Colorado Plateau.

265 Ponderosa Campground — For a picnic or extended overnight stay, the popular campground directly south of the highway is attractively laid out in a forest of thick ponderosa pines. Amenities include 61 campsites, picnic tables, grills, water, rest rooms, an RV dump station and a series of scenic hiking trails. A modest fee is charged. Closed September 30 to May 30.

267 Dude Fire Tour — Just before reaching this milepost, the paved Control Road (FR 64) parallels the Rim west to the small residential community of Tonto Village. This route also provides access to the area of the disastrous Dude fire, started by lightning near Dude Creek on June 2, 1990. The fire destroyed nearly 25,000 acres of timber. More than 2,600 firefighters were employed in suppressing it. Six lost their lives.

The ranger station in Payson offers a free, self-guided tour booklet that will direct you through the burnt region. Much of the tour is best driven in a high-clearance vehicle. Reach the area by driving to Tonto Village; proceed left on the dirt road (still FR 64), then turn right on FR 29.

Forest roads 64 and 65 will also take you to Diamond Point Lookout. The country is beautiful, and it's fun to look for "Arizona diamonds," quartz crystals that are sometimes found scattered in this general area. If the Forest Service gate is open, you may drive through and visit the lookout tower.

If you like to hike, FR 64 also winds its way west into the Highline National Recreation Trail Area, the spectacular country surrounding the 51-mile-long Highline Trail. Maps for the Highline may be obtained at ranger stations in the Rim area.

268 Kohl's Ranch — Beyond this milepost, a right turn takes you onto the grounds of Kohl's Ranch. Once a working cattle ranch, today it's a popular stop for high-country visitors. The ranch offers a rustic 50-unit motel with a restaurant, gift shop, and cocktail lounge. Horseback riding, fishing, swimming, and easy access to numerous mountain-hiking trails are also available.

Just past Kohl's Ranch on State Route 260, FR 289 winds north to the former site of the historic Zane Grey cabin where the famous Western author lived and wrote. Unfortunately, the cabin burned down during the Dude fire.

This road also leads to the Tonto Fish Hatchery. An interpretive walk explains the operation of the hatchery and permits you to view rainbow, brook, and brown trout, from fingerlings to fish that are ready to "plant" in nearby lakes and streams.

269 Camp Tontozona — Late summer brings the Sun Devil football team from Arizona State University to the cool pine country of Camp Tontozona to prepare for the fall season.

272 Christopher Creek Campground — This attractive 43-unit Forest Service campground just south of the highway on Christopher Creek offers picnic tables, grills, rest rooms, water, and trash collection. A modest overnight fee is charged. Closed from September 30 through May 30.

273 Village of Christopher Creek — This small community offers a service station, RV park, cabins in the pines, and groceries. The village, like the creek itself, is named for Isadore Christopher, a frontier rancher. In 1882, he killed a bear in the nearby woods, skinned it, and hung it in a frame outbuilding. While Christopher was away on business, an Apache raiding party swept through and torched the property. Troops arrived the next day, and, after poking through the burned buildings, found the charred bear carcass and assumed it was the deceased settler. A proper funeral was held. As the last clods were being thrown on the makeshift coffin, the rancher returned. Anyway, that's how the story goes. Be aware that some frontier tales, like caught fish, tend to grow with the passage of time.

278 260 Trailhead — This is the eastern terminus of the Highline Trail, the 51-mile pioneer route along the base of the Mogollon Rim. It is one of the state's most popular trails for hiking, horseback riding, and mountain bicycling.

279 Ascending the Mogollon Rim — Shortly after passing this milepost, you will begin an ascent of the Mogollon Rim. In early years, this part of Arizona was rife with wild game. Government lion hunters made their living by shooting the big cats that killed large numbers of cattle. Today the lions, with their numbers greatly diminished, are a subject of controversy. Environmentalists seek their protection; ranchers argue that there are still too many on the loose. Large herds of elk still wander the meadows and canyons here. The elk population is carefully monitored, and hunting permits are issued on a restricted basis.

282 Al Fulton Point — Just before passing this milepost you will leave the Tonto National Forest and enter Apache Sitgreaves National Forest. On the south side of State Route 260 is a large, paved parking area and visitor center.

This location, known as Al Fulton Point, provides a superb panoramic view from the very edge of the Mogollon Rim. Fulton was an early sheepman who was killed when his horse fell (some say stampeded) into a nearby sinkhole. East from the parking lot a trail leads three-quarters of a mile to Fulton's grave.

A paved road leads north (5 miles) to Woods Canyon Lake. Known as the Rim Lakes Recreation Area, there are several campgrounds and small high-country lakes in this vicinity.

Nick Berezenko

283 Willow Springs Lake — To the north is the turnoff to 80-acre Willow Springs Lake. This lake is man-made, deep, and stocked with rainbow and brown trout. A campground is within walking distance.

Aspen trees, identified by their white trunks and circular green leaves that "quake" in the breeze, begin to appear. Aspen grow in abundance above 8,000 feet, but a few have taken hold and are prospering here at about 7,600 feet.

In wet weather and after spring melt you'll find shallow Lake Number One to the south of the highway. In the 1870s, soldiers building Crook's Trail gave this lake a number instead of a name. It was a reliable water source for their horses, and thus a popular spot for cavalry and cowboys.

284 Road to Young — Beyond this milepost an unpaved road leads south through sparsely populated country to Pleasant Valley and the small community of Young. This country witnessed an extremely violent, long-lasting, 1880s feud between cattlemen and sheep raisers. More than 30 men were killed. Most nonparticipants in the Pleasant Valley War fled the region. After the end of hostilities in 1892, they slowly returned. Today the area is quiet, peaceful, and lives up to its Pleasant Valley name.

286 Canyon Point Campground — This large (117 units) campground at an elevation of 7,700 feet is a popular weekend escape for Arizona's desert dwellers. Because of its central location it is also ideal as a summer vacation "base camp" from which to take day trips.

288 Forest Lakes — At an elevation of 7,600 feet, Forest Lakes, built on the site of the 1880s Long Tom Ranch, is another Rim country vacation stop. The community offers a motel, cabins, a restaurant, canoe rentals, a ski shop, and other services. This region is known for its excellent cross-country skiing. Black Canyon Lake and campground are about 6 miles to the south.

Arizona Historical Society

289 The General Crook Trail — In 1871, in order to facilitate the movement of military supplies, Gen. George Crook laid out a wagon road that stretched more than 140 miles from Camp Verde to Fort Apache, about 30 miles south of Show Low. In its zigzag course across the top of the Rim, the old route crossed the highway numerous times, once near this point. Today it is designated a National Recreational Trail

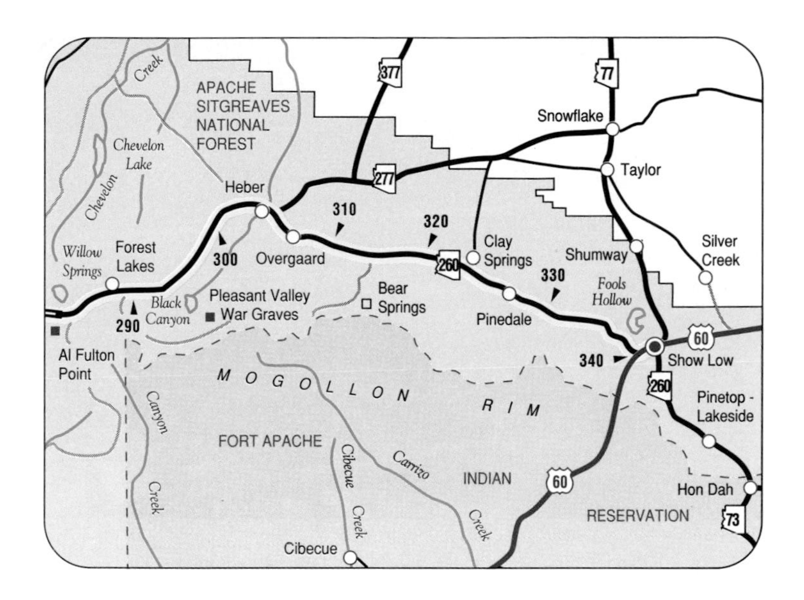

and is a favorite of warm-weather hikers and cross-country skiers. Contact the U.S. Forest Service for maps.

304 **Heber, Overgaard, and Apache Country** — Like many other small towns in northern Arizona, Heber was established by early Mormon settlers who migrated south from Utah during the last quarter of the 19th century. Heber is named for Heber C. Kimball, chief justice of the state of Deseret, which eventually became Utah. Overgaard's name is from a family in the area.

About 12 miles south of Heber/Overgaard the edge of the Mogollon Rim marks the northern boundary of the Fort Apache Indian Reservation, which stretches south and east across more than 5,000 square miles. The tribe, once known for its fierce warriors, today is prosperously engaged in lumbering, ranching, farming, and tourism. Its Sunrise Ski Resort is one of the most popular in the Southwest.

312 **Bear Springs, Pleasant Valley War Lynching** — Bear Springs, about 4 miles south of the highway, got its name in 1885. Cowboys on a roundup, so the story goes, roped a bear at these springs.

The place was also part of the Circle Dot Ranch, owned by James Stott, a young man from a well-to-do Massachusetts family. In August of 1887, Deputy Sheriff J.D. Houck and a small posse arrested Stott and two companions, James Scott and Billy Wilson, at the ranch. Charged with horse stealing, the handcuffed men

Nick Berezenko

rode west with the posse. Some miles later, a much larger vigilante band abducted the three, ran off Deputy Houck's group, and lynched the suspects from a ponderosa pine.

The Pleasant Valley War was a family feud and cattleman-sheepman range war. It lasted for more than a decade and blurred the lines of right and wrong, good and bad. The excuse for the lynching was that Stott, Scott, and Wilson were horse thieves. Truth be told, it is likely that Stott's only offense was owning range and water the vigilantes wanted. Scott and Wilson may have been disreputable, having enjoyed the companionship of individuals of questionable character. However, on that particular day, they probably just happened to be in the wrong place at the wrong time.

320 **View of the White Mountains** — Beyond this milepost a downhill incline provides a good view of the distant horizon. At a 1 o'clock position, note a dip in the near horizon and the faint blue outline of distant mountains beyond. Those blue silhouettes are the high ridges of Arizona's magnificent White Mountain region. From this point, the tallest is McKays Peak, 9,220 feet in elevation. Beyond, but not visible, is Mount Baldy, the state's second highest mountain at 11,590 feet.

337 **Show Low City Limits** — Show Low takes its name from an 1876 winner-take-all card game between Corydon Cooley, a noted Indian scout, and Marion Clark. The two had established a large ranch in the area, but differences between them dictated a split in the partnership. They decided to settle the matter with a game of cards. After several hours of play, Clark

suggested they each turn a single card. "Show low and you win," said Clark. Cooley did — with the deuce of clubs — and the matter was settled.

338 Fools Hollow Lake — This popular local lake just north of the highway is known for its trout, bass, bluegill, and catfish. There are free campgrounds on two shores and a boat ramp, but no drinking water. Closed from October 1 through May 1. The location got its name because an early settler attempted, unsuccessfully, to grow crops in the rocky terrain.

340 Downtown Show Low — East of the intersection of State Route 260 and U.S. 60 is the business district of Show Low. For many years Show Low has catered to four seasons of tourist trade, so the community offers a wide and attractive range of lodging, restaurants, and retail services.

If you intend to continue through Arizona's White Mountain Country, or travel south towards Globe, you will intersect Tour Fifteen (see page 195) at this point.

TOUR PHOTOGRAPHS BY DAVID ELMS, JR.

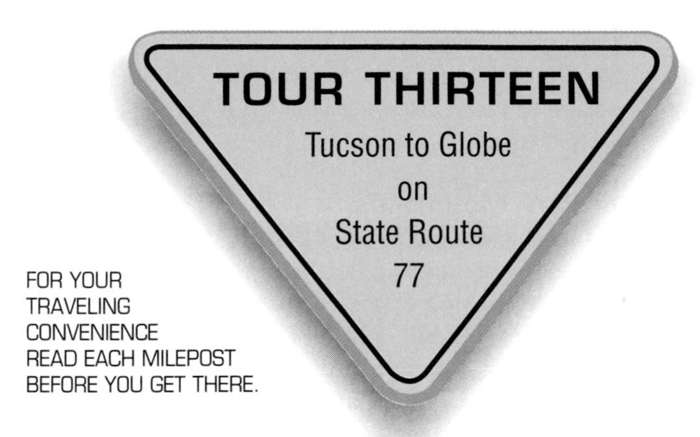

FOR YOUR TRAVELING CONVENIENCE READ EACH MILEPOST BEFORE YOU GET THERE.

Starting Point — Your journey starts in Tucson. For a brief profile of this intriguing city turn to page 77.

Along the Way — This 105-mile journey takes you from the cultural climate of the Old Pueblo, around the Santa Catalina Mountains, north through lush Sonoran desert, deep canyons of the Gila River, and on to the historic mining community of Globe.

Along the way, you will view the region where the legendary Mine with the Iron Door is supposedly located; view a smelter stack as tall as a 100-story skyscraper; and travel through country so rugged that a frontier general advised all who contemplated a westward journey to avoid it.

Mileposts for this trip will be in ascending order.

MILEPOST HIGHLIGHTS

State Route 77 North from Tucson — Your auto tour from Tucson to Globe conveniently starts on State Route 77. For those new to the Tucson area, State Route 77 is also called Miracle Mile and Oracle Road in town. Go north.

Rillito River (Creek) — Different maps list different names — Rillito river, creek, or wash. Nevertheless, beyond this milepost, you will cross a "river" with a redundant name. Translated from Spanish, *rillito* (ree-yee-toe) means "small river." Very little water flows in the channel, but infrequent cloudbursts send torrents of water rushing along its course.

(Left) The lights of Tucson come on as an autumn evening settles over the city. The Santa Catalina Mountains are in the background.

In 1872 the army post of Fort Lowell was relocated from its downtown site to the outlying banks of the Rillito. The move reportedly was made to protect the soldiers from Tucson's dangerously rowdy civilians.

73 Santa Catalina Mountains — This massive range of mountains east of the highway consists of a fore range of rocks formed by the ancient cooling of molten magma, which was later tilted upward by the wrenching of the earth. Behind the fore range is a larger dome of granite, uplifted about 50 million years ago. As you proceed north, the division between the fore range and the dome will become more apparent.

75 Desert Flora — Landscaping on the median provides a sampling of the plants of Arizona's lower Sonoran Desert. Cactus with flat, pancake-like leaves are prickly pear. Barrel cactus are short, rounded and usually under three feet tall. Cholla have numerous, jointed arms with sharp, yellowish needles. Agave plants consist of a clump of heavy, gray-green upthrusting leaves that are stiff and as sharp as daggers. Ocotillo are tall clumps of thorny sticks that sometimes have small leaves and red flowers. Young paloverde trees display a smooth bark with green limbs. Also on the median, you will see some young saguaros displaying only a single trunk covered with spines. Older saguaros rise above 20 feet and usually have numerous arms.

78 Mount Lemmon — Now the division between the craggy fore range of the Santa Catalinas and the larger granite dome can be more easily seen. The highest point on the dome is Mount Lemmon at an elevation of 9,157 feet. The area, thick in pine, fir, and aspen, is a popular summer vacation spot. Winter brings crowds to this southernmost ski area in North America.

79 Pusch Ridge — The rocky promontory to the east is Pusch Ridge. It takes its name from George Pusch, who was born in Germany in the mid-1800s, arrived in Tucson in 1876, and

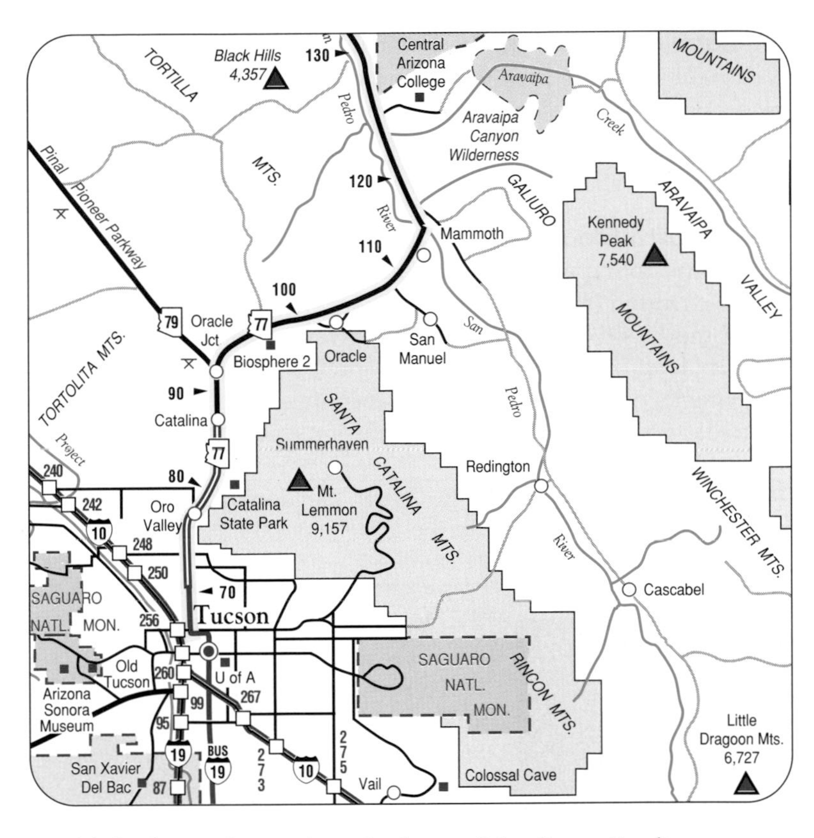

established a cattle ranch at the base of the Santa Catalina Mountains near this ridge.

80 Cañada Del Oro — Beyond this milepost a bridge crosses Cañada del Oro ("canyon of gold"), so named because of some promising frontier mineral discoveries. The location is best known as the site where, in 1894, prospector John Scanlon claimed to have killed the notorious Apache Kid. The Kid, once a trusted government scout, was convicted of a crime he may not have committed. While being transported to prison he escaped. Later, the "dead or alive" reward rose to more than $5,000. Scanlon was unable to produce the Kid's body, so he received no reward. The wily former scout was never apprehended. Some reports claim that he fled to Mexico, where he lived well into the 20th century.

Arizona Dept. of Library & Archives

81 Catalina State Park — Located adjacent to Coronado National Forest, the park provides a visitor center, campsites, and picnic areas with tables, grills, drinking water, and rest rooms. Modest entry fee. The 5,500-acre area offers hiking, horseback riding, and nature study in a rugged foothill setting.

85 Tortolita Mountains — These small, uplifted granite mountains on the west side are known for their enhancing name change. During frontier times they were (for reasons unknown) called the Bloodsucker Mountains. However, someone (perhaps an early land developer with a public relations problem) noticed large flocks of doves in the area and changed the name to Tortolita, which translated from Spanish means "little turtle dove."

91 Oracle Junction — At Oracle Junction, which was established as a stage stop in the 1880s, take the fork to the east (right) and proceed on State Route 77.

92 Yucca Plants — For many miles ahead you will see stands of yucca that display a large cluster of long, narrow, pointed leaves. Sometimes the cluster is close to the ground; sometimes it sits on a thick, gray trunk. Frequently the plants sport a tall flower stalk. Yucca plants were a valuable resource, providing food and fiber for Native Americans. The leaves were stripped and woven into baskets and sandals; yucca roots were used to make soap.

94 The Mine with the Iron Door — Look to the south. Legend has it that early Spaniards mined rich veins of gold in one of the remote canyons on the north slopes of the Santa Catalinas, then stored the smelted bars in a cave sealed by an iron door. The location was lost when the miners were wiped out by raiding Apaches. For well over a century, gold seekers have searched for the mine without success.

96 Biosphere 2 — Beyond this milepost is the entrance to the largest man-made, self-sustaining ecosystem ever constructed. Under three acres of steel and glass, Biosphere 2 contains a rain forest, savanna, marsh, ocean, desert, farm, and living quarters. In December of 1991, eight researchers were sealed inside to live and work for two years without physical contact with the outside world. One of the purposes of the experiment is to determine methods for establishing colonies on distant planets. Tours of surrounding facilities are available to the public. Call ahead for a tour reservation (602-825-6222). There is a fee. A motel and restaurant are located at the site.

100 Oracle — This name is derived from a ship, *The Oracle*, on which Albert Weldon sailed around the Horn in 1875. Weldon built a brush camp while assessing the Oracle Mine in 1880. Now located at a different site, Oracle is a modern-day version of rural, small-town America with a modest business district, several churches, and homes scattered in the wooded hills.

One of Oracle's most energetic frontier citizens was "Curly Bill" Neal, son of a black father and Cherokee mother. Neal arrived in the last quarter of the 19th century and opened a successful freight-hauling business. This was followed by an equally successful stage line. Then he took up ranching and soon was running thousands of cattle. In 1895 he branched out again and opened the Mountain View Hotel, which caught on as a popular vacation resort. Curly Bill died in 1936. Today the renovated hotel serves as a church.

103 San Pedro Valley — The tree-lined valley directly ahead was created by the San Pedro River. Starting in Mexico, this north-flowing river courses its way across nearly 150 miles of Arizona before joining the Gila River about 20 miles north of here.

104 Galiuro Mountains — The rugged range directly ahead remains one of the most primitive regions in the Southwest. The name Galiuro has no translatable meaning and was the result of a series of mistakes. The earliest name was the Spanish Salitre (nitrate). A later map spells the name Calitre. A subsequent version shows the "e" changed to "o," resulting in Calitro. Still later, a cartographer changed the "t" to "u," and thereafter the name appeared as Caliuro until, finally, the "C," became "G," giving the range its present name.

109 San Manuel Mining Operations — Just beyond the turnoff to San Manuel, at a 2 o'clock position, you can see evidence of Magma Copper Company's extensive mining activities. The white tailings dump and the emerald-green pond are the result of milling operations that began in 1954. The mines are capable of producing nearly 300,000 tons of copper each year. Of the two smelter stacks visible, the tallest is 550 feet. About 20 miles ahead, you will see a stack nearly twice as tall.

113 Mammoth — With the discovery of ore veins of mammoth proportions, this small community was given its name in the 1870s. Today Mammoth is a quiet community where some of the adobe buildings date back to the town's earliest days.

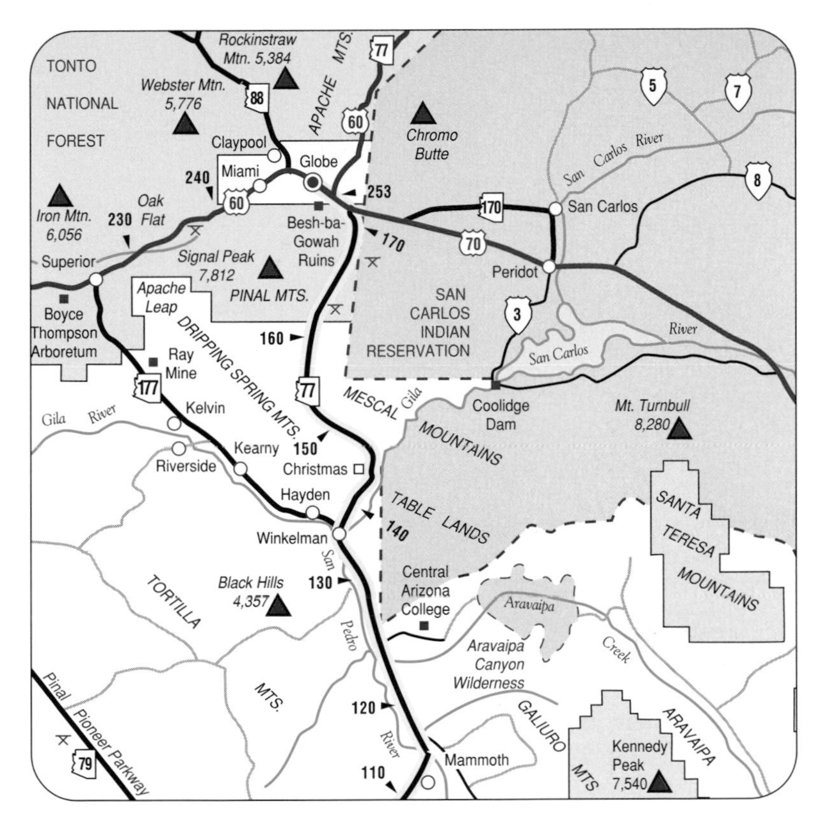

116 San Pedro River Crossing — Although the San Pedro runs shallow most of the time, it was once populated by large numbers of beavers — so many, in fact, that early trappers called it "Beaver River." The jungle of trees along the river's course are mostly mesquite.

117 Saguaro Cactus — The hills east of the highway are covered with stately saguaro cactus. The tallest living specimen, located in the Maricopa Mountains west of Casa Grande, stands 57 feet, 11 inches tall. Most saguaros stand about 30 feet tall.

123 Aravaipa Creek — In May of 1860 Fort Aravaipa was established near here. It's hard to believe that the name, which means "girls," was given to the Aravaipa Apaches for some "unmanly deed," because they held sway over the entire area from Mexico to the Gila River prior to 1853. To the east, the waters of Aravaipa Creek emerge from the rugged, high-walled Aravaipa Canyon Wilderness. Although not very long, it is one of the few perennial streams in the Southwest. Fremont cottonwood trees are plentiful along the wash and native to the region.

132 Smelter Stacks — Straight ahead are a pair of impressive stacks at the ASARCO copper mining and smelting site. Located near the community of Hayden, the taller stack rises 1,000 feet, almost equal to the height of a 100-story skyscraper. Because of surrounding mountains, the extreme height is necessary to take advantage of winds that carry away the discharge.

134 Junction of State Route 177 — Near this milepost you enter the mining community of Winkelman and cross the Gila River. The Gila flows out of the highlands of New Mexico and across the entire 400-mile width of Arizona to meet the Colorado River at the state's western border. Take the fork to the east (right) to continue on to Globe.

139 Canyons of the Gila River — Modern engineering techniques make your route through the Gila River's canyons possible. But in 1846, Gen. Stephen Kearny found this region so unsuited for wheeled vehicles that he advised against any attempts to build transportation routes along this section of the Gila. His advice was taken and the Butterfield Stage Route, the Southern Pacific Railroad, the first U.S. highways, and modern Interstate 10 all swing south to avoid this extremely rugged country. Today, the Gila's waters are impounded behind Coolidge Dam about 25 miles northeast.

140 Twisted Rock Formations — Note the exposed layers of tilted rock east of the highway. Hundreds of millions of years ago these sedimentary formations lay almost perfectly flat, but the heaving and buckling of the earth created these wildly tossed ridges, a common sight in the mountain regions of the Southwest.

145 Christmas — There are several versions of who gave the old mining camp of Christmas its name. Dr. James Douglas and two prospectors are said to have discovered copper here in the early 1880s, but could not claim it because it was part of the San Carlos Indian Reservation.

Later George Chittenden managed to have Congress pass a bill changing the reservation boundary lines. News of the change arrived via telegraph on his birthday, Christmas 1902.

Or — the mine was located by a Mike O'Brien, purchased by Chittenden, and the post office named Christmas in 1905 by a school teacher.

Or — Albert Weldon (see Milepost 100 Oracle), Alex McKay, and Jimmy Lee located the mine during the Christmas season of 1881 and so named it, hoping Santa Clause would bring them a great present.

As of this printing, roads into Christmas are closed and the signs read, "Cyrus Christmas Corp. No Trespassing."

152 Jesus Rock — Different people see different things in the shapes of rocks. One of the most common is Snoopy, from the comic strip *Peanuts*. But between mileposts 152 and 153, on the east side of the road, is a geologic figure known to locals as Jesus Rock. It is particularly easy for north-bound travelers to spot.

155 It's Not Anyone's Fault — At first glance, this large gash in the hillside appears to be an ominous fault line. It is actually a slot canyon, a geological feature common 300 miles to the north, but rarely found on Arizona's southern desert. As mentioned in Milepost 140, titanic forces long ago caused layers of fine-grain sedimentary rock to fold and buckle up. A naturally occurring crack in the vertical strata, and the steep gradient, then allowed rain water to erode out the slot canyon.

158 Changing Geographical Life Zones — You are now climbing above 4,000 feet, moving from the lower Sonoran zone into the upper Sonoran zone. Within the next 3 miles, the surrounding hillsides will be above 5,000 feet. The saguaros will disappear and be replaced by oak, juniper, and piñon pine, with a few sycamores along washes.

162 El Capitan Pass and Rest Area — This stop provides ramadas, picnic tables, and a panoramic view of the 5,467-square-mile expanse of the San Carlos Apache and Fort Apache Indian reservations that stretch north and east far beyond the horizon.

169 Pinal Mountains and Signal Peak — Beyond this milepost you will follow a sweeping curve that provides an excellent view of the Pinal Mountains to the west. Signal Peak (7,812 feet), the highest point in this popular camping and hiking area, was once part of a chain of frontier heliograph stations that extended from central Arizona all the way to Texas. This method of sending messages by reflected sunlight permitted the Army to communicate across hundreds of miles in a matter of minutes. The "modern" technology mystified and confused Geronimo and his renegade Apache warriors, and ultimately led to their capture.

171 Junction with U.S. Highway 70 — Turn west on U.S. 70 and drive 3 miles into Globe to conclude your milepost tour. In the early 1900s Globe's Old Dominion Mine flourished as one of the world's largest copper mines, but the deposits played out in the '30s and the mine closed. Today Globe is a repository of frontier history and a pleasant place to stop. The Chamber of Commerce provides maps for self-guided mine tours and a walking tour of the historic downtown area. Besh-ba-Gowah Ruins is an archeological site where more than 200 rooms of the prehistoric Salado culture have been discovered and preserved (modest admission fee).

TOUR PHOTOGRAPHS BY DAVID ELMS, JR.

FOR YOUR TRAVELING CONVENIENCE READ EACH MILEPOST BEFORE YOU GET THERE.

Starting Point — This milepost trek begins in the community of Apache Junction. This starting point, approximately 35 miles east of downtown Phoenix, can be reached by traveling east on the Superstition Freeway (U.S. 60), or east of Mesa on Apache Boulevard.

A few decades ago, Apache Junction was only a gas station at a fork in the road. But in recent years, an influx of desert dwellers has transformed the area into a sizable community. Situated at the base of the legendary Superstition Mountains, Apache Junction is best known as the gateway to the Apache Trail (State Route 88), a historic, mostly dirt road that twists above spectacular canyons as it wends its way through Arizona's desert lakes region.

In the immediate vicinity of Apache Junction, Lost Dutchman State Park offers camping, hiking, and some impressive views of the massive Superstitions. You can also rent horses, dine at a variety of restaurants, and pick from a wide selection of lodging accommodations. For more information, stop by the visitor center at Apache Junction City Hall.

Along the Way — This is a short 57-mile tour that offers impressively rugged desert scenery, tempting side trips, and a wealth of history. You will skirt the Superstition Wilderness, nearly 160,000 acres of some of the most beautiful but inhospitable country on the continent, climb steeply into a land of deep gorges and strangely sculpted rock formations, visit one of the nation's most interesting arboretums, and tour the historic sites of some of the Southwest's richest copper mines.

Mileposts will be in ascending order.

(Left) Between Oak Flat, Milepost 230, and Top of the World, Milepost 235, U.S. Route 60 twists and turns through a wonderland of rocks.

MILEPOST HIGHLIGHTS

MILE 197 **Superstition Mountains** — The massive mountains looming to the east were born amid riotous volcanic activity 15-35 million years ago. More than 2,500 cubic miles of lava and ash were spewed out across the prehistoric landscape. The ash was so hot it welded itself into the strangely contorted formations of volcanic tuff that abound in the region. The roofs of the then empty magma chambers collapsed, forming giant calderas. These in turn were filled by upthrusts of lava, which created the resurgent dome that is seen today. The jagged formations seen here are some of the earliest that were formed.

199 **Silly Mountain** — Just south of the Superstition Freeway is Silly Mountain Road and just east of the highway is Silly Mountain itself, a rugged little desert peak with an incredibly steep road to the summit. Local folks say it was named for people silly enough to try driving to the top. The road offers an intimidating incline, but people with four-wheel-drive vehicles frequently take the test. We advise against it.

200 **Flora of the Lower Sonoran Desert** — Here the landscape grows lush with plant life of the lower Sonoran Desert. Most prevalent among the cactus are cholla (whitish, many-jointed with needle-sharp thorns), saguaro (sometimes over 30 feet in height with extended arms), and short, stubby barrel cactus. Low-growing trees are mesquite (dark, rough bark) or paloverde, with smoother bark and light green limbs.

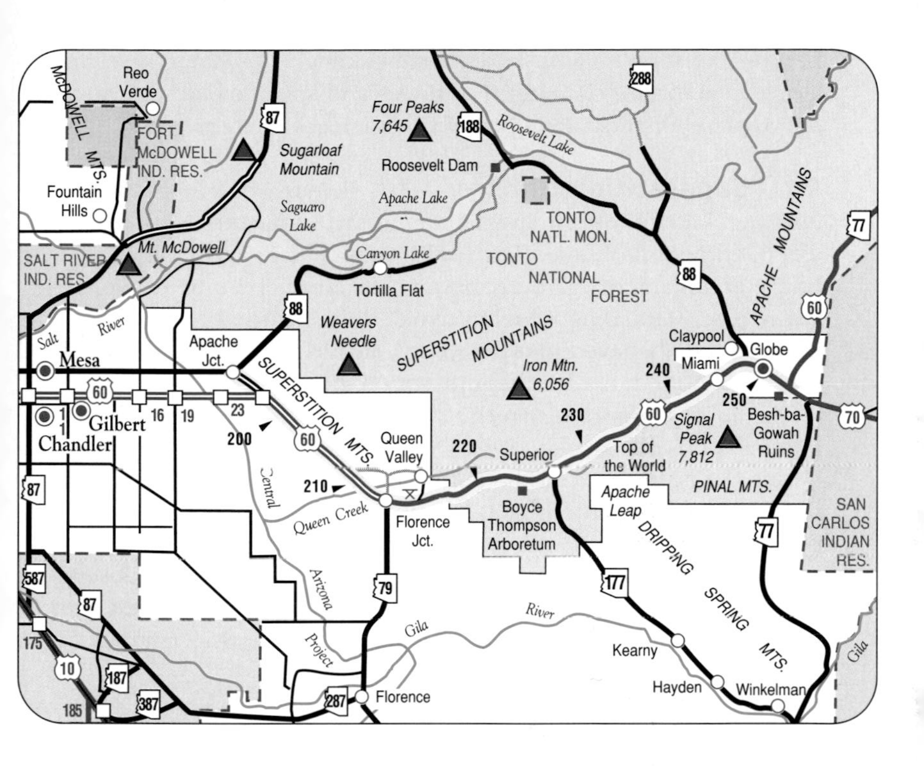

202 Mountain Brook Village, Gold Canyon Ranch — Tucked away in low foothills a half-mile to the east is the retirement and leisure-living community of Mountain Brook Village. The village is a good demonstration of the non-urban, semi-secluded lifestyle that is popular in Arizona. Before Milepost 203 you will reach Kings Ranch Road and the entrance to Gold Canyon Ranch, a sprawling resort and conference center with a fastidiously manicured 18-hole golf course. The golf course and restaurant are open to the public. There is a riding stable nearby.

204 Road to Peralta Trailhead — This road leads to one of Arizona's favorite hiking trails. Seven miles to the east, the Peralta Trail winds 2.3 miles through wild canyons of the Superstitions to Fremont Saddle and a close-up view of the immense spire of Weaver's Needle. This ancient volcanic core, nearly 1,300 feet in height, is said to be a key landmark in locating the Lost Dutchman mine. If you go, wear hiking shoes and carry plenty of water.

205 Renaissance Festival — On weekends in February and March the Middle Ages come to life on the Arizona desert. This storybook village featuring jugglers, artisans, nobles, beggars, jousting knights, and swashbuckling swordsmen — even a medieval torture chamber. For prices and specific dates contact the Apache Junction Chamber of Commerce.

210 **Superstition Ghosts** — E.A. Reavis was one of the few men known to have lived alone in the Superstitions for any extended period of time. From 1871 until 1896 Reavis built a house and planted a garden and orchard far back in the canyons to the east. Marauding Apaches avoided the bearded hermit because they believed him possessed. Reavis, who died of natural causes, is buried in a lonely Superstition grave.

The Superstitions are also the site of the Lost Dutchman gold mine. Supposedly worked by a Dutchman named Jacob Waltz during the last quarter of the 19th century, the mine has been sought since his death in 1891. Stories of buried Spanish gold, bushwhacked prospectors, stolen maps, and skeletons found in lonely canyons are almost as numerous as saguaros on the desert.

Disappointingly, the U.S. Bureau of Mines states that there is no evidence of any gold-bearing formations in the Superstitions.

211 **Queen Creek** — Just before Milepost 211, Queen Creek, usually only a dry stream bed but a raging torrent after thunderstorms, twists down from higher elevations to the east. Beyond the mining town of Superior you will cross Queen Creek again, but in a deep and rugged canyon bordered by soaring rock formations.

212 **Junction with State Route 79** — While your tour continues east on U.S. Highway 60, State Route 79 aims almost directly south toward the community of Florence, then on to Tucson. The 40-mile stretch south of Florence to Oracle Junction is called Pinal Pioneer Parkway. It is especially noted for its picnic table pull-outs, and in spring, its beautiful collection of signed roadside plants.

214 **Roadside Rest Area** — A roadside stop on the north side of the highway near this milepost provides rest rooms, water, and picnic tables. Past the rest area, a paved road goes north 4 miles to Queen Valley, a retirement village of mobile homes, RVs, and small houses in a picturesque desert setting.

215 **Weaver's Needle** — Beyond this milepost, get ready for an excellent view of the huge, upthrusting spire of Weaver's Needle. As the highway curves to the left, look to the northern horizon (9 o'clock position). This tall, thumb-shaped pinnacle

supposedly casts a shadow across the shaft of the Lost Dutchman Mine. However, people have been following the shadow for a century without locating the mine.

217 **Tonto National Forest** — Near this milepost you enter Tonto National Forest. While the vegetation at this point is not typically forested, be aware that this dedicated area stretches across nearly 3 million acres and includes numerous pine-covered peaks approaching 8,000 feet.

218 **Gonzales Pass** — In the early 1870s silver was discovered in the Globe area, causing the government to delete a 12-mile strip of land from the San Carlos Indian Reservation and give it up for mining development. But the Indians were so ferocious, the mountains so steep, the canyons so deep, and the entire region so remote that progress was impossible. The silver only lasted four years, but by then rich copper ore emerged.

Fear of Indian attacks eased only slightly in 1886 when Geronimo surrendered. For the next 20 years supplies were brought from New Mexico by mule. A railroad spur was extended from Bowie in southern Arizona in 1898. In 1910, the first tortuous dirt road between Phoenix and Globe was via the Apache Trail and Roosevelt Dam.

Not until 1922 did a highway from Phoenix conveniently link Superior, Miami, and Globe. Gonzales Pass? It's named after Juan Gonzales, one of the hardy, early-day freighters to use this route.

223 Boyce Thompson Southwestern Arboretum — You are approaching the entrance to one of the world's largest displays of desert plants. It was established in the early 1920s by mining magnate and botanical enthusiast William Boyce Thompson. More than 1,500 types of desert plants, including many rare ones, grow on the arboretum's 1,200 acres. Located in a deep canyon, there is a picnic area, walking paths, and much of the area is shaded by towering trees and erosion-carved cliffs. The arboretum is administered by the Arizona State Parks Department. There is an admission fee.

On Route 60, beyond the arboretum, an historical marker provides information on Picket Post Mountain. This malformed peak, just south of the highway, consists of a cap of lava over thick layers of compacted volcanic ash (tuff). During frontier periods of Apache conflict, the summit was used as a lookout point and heliograph station.

226 Town of Superior and Apache Leap — In 1900 when George Lobb laid out the town site, the operations were owned by the Arizona and Lake Superior Mining Company, hence the tent city's name. Then in 1914, the Magma Copper Company built a huge smelter and Superior grew rapidly. North of town are the visible remains of the Magma Copper Mine. Some of Superior's underground mines are 3,000 feet below the highway.

The Dripping Spring Mountains are directly ahead and beyond the town. Their sheer cliffs were the alleged site of a tragic frontier encounter between soldiers and Apaches. Seventy-five warriors, so the story goes, were trapped at the top of the precipice and chose to jump to their deaths rather than surrender. Thus the name Apache Leap.

228 Queen Creek Bridge and Tunnel — Remember crossing Queen Creek on the flat desert floor near Milepost 211? Just before reaching Milepost 228 you will cross it again, but this time it winds through the bottom of Queen Canyon, which is

bordered on both sides by mountains of heavily eroded stone.

The canyon was a daunting challenge for highway engineers. In 1922, the first road up the canyon included a small tunnel (watch closely, it's to the canyon side of the present one). Then in 1952 they constructed the new 1,149-foot-long Queen Creek Tunnel, and the 651-foot steel bridge.

At the lower end of the tunnel you may notice sedimentary rocks overlayed by welded tuff, which is brittle and highly fractured. At the upper end, you will notice the tuff has eroded into sharp ridges and towers.

235 Top of the World — In the 1950s the old highway used to wind its way past the Top of the World guest ranch. Looking plain on the outside and like a casino on the inside, the ranch was not noted for its working cowboys, but rather its "working girls." Today, at an elevation approaching 5,000 feet, the restful little valley is dotted with a few mobile homes tucked between giant boulders, small buildings under shady oak trees, and roadside enterprises.

236 Changing Geographical Zone — You are now at an elevation above 4,500 feet. This altitude is an approximate demarcation point between the lower and upper Sonoran zones. Note that desert growth has been replaced by heavy stands of oak, juniper and piñon pine.

237 Pinto Valley Mine — Looking to the north, you can see the massive, open-pit Pinto Valley Copper Mine. Worked since the early 1940s, the mine has produced more than 2 billion pounds of copper. Rock is blasted from the pit, crushed, and then chemically processed. A ton of raw ore produces only six pounds of copper. Beyond Milepost 239, a road to the area permits a closer look at the mine.

242 Bloody Tanks Wash — You are now entering an area where huge tailing dumps and old mine buildings provide evidence of mining operations that stretch back more than a century. Near this milepost you cross Bloody Tanks Wash where a roadside rest area is located just north of the highway.

In 1864, at a water tank up the wash, a group of militiamen led by a frontier character named King Woolsey persuaded a group of Apache Indians to attend a peace powwow. After the Indians had accepted gifts of food and tobacco, Woolsey's men massacred them. It is said that the bloody encounter inspired the grim name.

244 Passing through Miami — The debris of long-term mining activity, including slag dumps (black material), tailing dumps (light material), and numerous operational buildings (many of them closed) litter the area. For example, just north of the highway, a power generating plant, the large abandoned building with the two tall stacks, once supplied electricity for underground and milling operations. The old headframe up on the hill marks the entrance to a labyrinth of deep mine shafts and tunnels.

247 Roosevelt Lake or the Pinal Mountains — At the junction of U.S. 60 and State Route 88, you have a choice of side trips if your schedule permits.

James Tallon

North 29 miles on State Route 88, you'll find the world's highest masonry dam, which impounds Roosevelt Lake's 20,000 surface-acres of water. In the same area, you can visit the well-preserved cliff dwellings of Tonto National Monument (modest entry fee). It is estimated that about 12,000 prehistoric Salado Indians once populated the valley and hillsides near today's Roosevelt Lake.

The road south at this junction leads to the Pinal Mountain Recreation Area in the heavily forested 7,812-foot Pinal Mountains. The area, about 10 miles away on a well-maintained gravel road, offers high-country campsites (some with facilities), picnic areas, and sweeping vistas of this part of Arizona.

248 The Historic Town of Globe — Situated in rugged, mineral-rich mountains, Globe was a true frontier boom town. Its richest mine, the Old Dominion (north of the highway) produced more than $135 million in gold, silver, and copper before its closing in the 1930s. During Arizona's early years, Globe's mineral wealth also made it a major center of political power.

Globe is rich in history. We suggest a stop at the Globe-Miami Chamber of Commerce (east of this milepost on the south side of the highway) for tour maps of the city and nearby mine sites. The Gila County Historical Museum (admission free), which covers local history back to prehistoric times, is located next to the Chamber of Commerce.

251 Besh-ba-Gowah Indian Ruins — Past this milepost a sign indicates the route to the extensive remains of a 13th-century Salado Indian village. More than 200 rooms have been discovered at this site. Some of the restored buildings contain authentic pottery, baskets, and household implements that accurately depict the period of occupation. The Salado were accomplished farmers, weavers, and pottery makers, but about A.D. 1400 they mysteriously disappeared. There is a small admission fee.

252 End of Tour — Near this milepost is the junction of three major highways. U.S. Highway 60 heads northeast to White Mountain country. If you are continuing on U.S. 60, see page 189 for a milepost tour that takes you from this point to Springerville. U.S. Route 70 heads southeast to Safford and on to the New Mexico border. And State Route 77, profiled as a milepost tour on page 167, goes south toward the majestic Santa Catalina Mountains and Tucson.

FOR YOUR TRAVELING CONVENIENCE READ EACH MILEPOST BEFORE YOU GET THERE.

Starting Point — The community of Globe was named for an immense globe-shaped nugget of silver found by a prospector in 1875. While the local veins of gold and silver were impressive, copper eventually became the primary product of the area. For a profile of Globe, turn to page 186, Mileposts 248 and 251.

Along the Way — This 136-mile trip climbs from Arizona's corrugated central highlands to heavily forested country above the cliffs of the Mogollon Rim.

You will pass through rugged, semi-arid mountains that attracted hordes of prospectors in the 1800s. The route descends into the erosion-carved depths of Salt River Canyon and through the sparsely populated Fort Apache Indian Reservation, an area of more than 1.5 million acres. At higher elevations, you will drive through part of America's largest ponderosa pine forest, then across plateau country dotted with ancient volcanic cinder cones.

The tour ends in Springerville, which, at an elevation of 7,000 feet, is a gateway community to Arizona's majestic White Mountain recreation area.

Mileposts are in ascending order.

MILEPOST HIGHLIGHTS

Junction U.S. 60 and U.S. 70 — East of downtown Globe near this milepost on U.S. Route 60 is a junction with U.S. 70, which runs southeast to Safford. At this same junction, State Route 77 goes south toward Tucson. However, to start your milepost tour, turn north on U.S. 60 at the traffic light.

(Left) Go slow and use lower gears when descending into scenic Salt River Canyon. The bridge is at Milepost 293.

257 Transition Zone Vegetation — Just beyond this milepost you will see desert mesquite trees (leafy and light green) and juniper trees (thick foliage, dark green) growing in the same broad areas because, at an elevation of 4,000 feet, you are at a transition point between the mesquite's lower Sonoran zone and the juniper's upper Sonoran zone.

258 Tonto National Forest — A few hundred yards ahead you enter Tonto National Forest. To the northwest the Tonto includes impressive pine forests and the Mogollon Rim. The Rim's nearly sheer escarpment forms the demarcation line between Arizona's central highlands (south of the Rim) and the uplifted land of the Colorado Plateau (north of the Rim). Directly east of the highway and stretching across more than 2,000 square miles are the San Carlos and Fort Apache Indian reservations.

260 Apache Mountains — The small, rounded peaks west of the highway are the Apache Mountains, logically named by the Wheeler expedition of 1869 because the area was a stronghold of the Apache Indians. Several military engagements with the Apaches occurred here in the early 1870s. To the immediate east is Chromo Butte, an abandoned site where chromo (mineral coloring used in dyes and paints) was once mined.

265 McMillanville — Just before this milepost, on the west side of the highway, is an historical marker denoting the road to the ghost town of McMillanville. With the discovery of the Stonewall Jackson silver ledge in 1874, McMillanville boomed overnight. But the deposits were soon depleted, and 10 years after its founding, only one person remained.

268 Jackson Butte — Immediately northwest is Jackson Butte (elevation 6,106 feet), a rather prominent peak that has no connection with the Stonewall Jackson silver ledge. It was thus named simply because a pioneer named Jackson raised livestock in the area. On the east side of the road is Jones Water Campground, a rather primitive spot that provides grills, tables, and sites for tents and RVs. It was named for an early rancher.

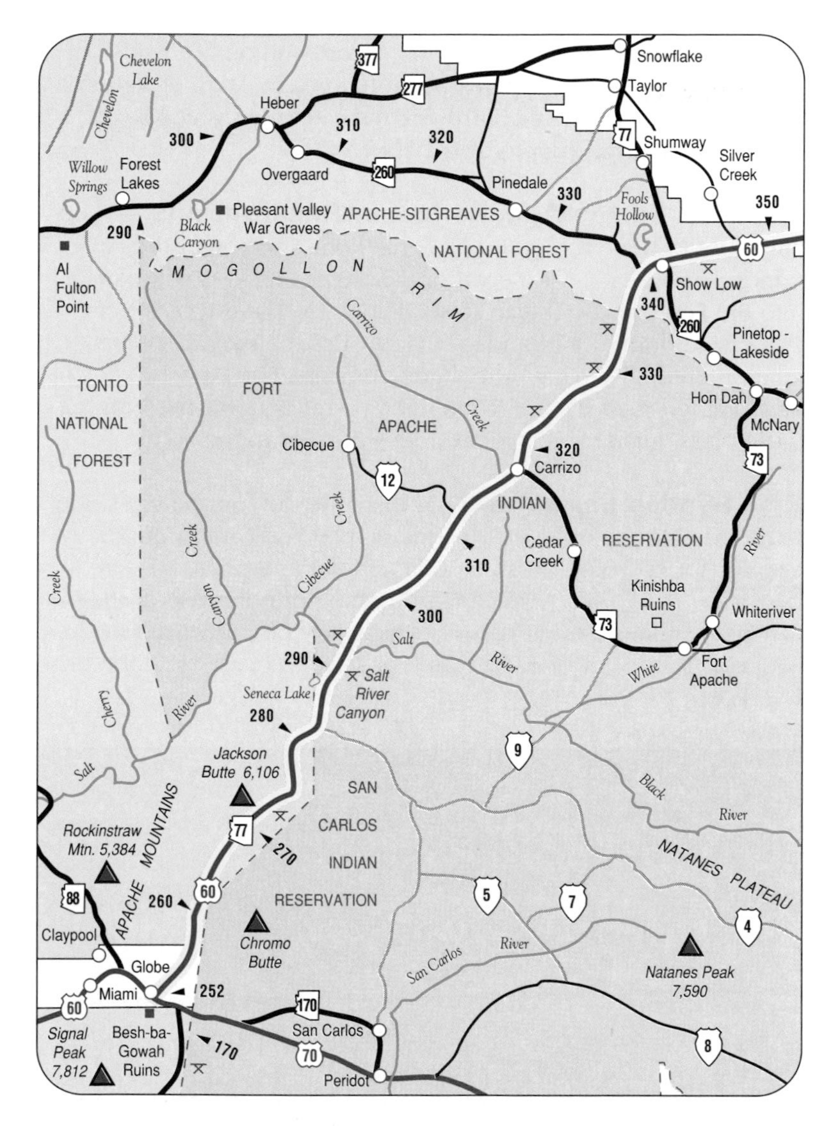

272 Roadside Rest Area — Past this milepost is a roadside rest area under sheltering oak trees that provides rest rooms and picnic tables.

277 Mazatzal Mountains — As the road bends north, look far to the west. Outlined against the sky are the distinctive Four Peaks of the Mazatzal Mountains, one of Arizona's more rugged wildernesses. Between your present location and these prominent landmarks there is little evidence of human habitation. Yet, not far beyond Four Peaks lies the Valley of the Sun and its suburban communities with a combined population approaching 2 million.

279 Ponderosa Pines — Not far ahead, and on both sides of the highway, ponderosa pines begin to appear. At an elevation nearing 6,000 feet, their occurrence indicates a transition point into yet another geographical life zone.

284 San Carlos Apache Indian Reservations — You are about to leave the Tonto National Forest and enter the San Carlos Apache Indian Reservation. Farther north you will pass into the Fort Apache Indian Reservation. The Salt River and the Black River form the boundary that divides the two. They are administered by separate tribal governments. Fort Apache's headquarters is located at Whiteriver, 30 miles northeast. San Carlos' headquarters is at San Carlos, 30 miles to the south.

287 Seneca Lake — Beyond this milepost, on the west side of the road, is the entrance to Seneca Lake and campground. Popular for its trout, catfish, and largemouth bass, this 27-acre lake is on San Carlos Apache land. Fishing or other use of the facilities requires a tribal permit, which may be purchased in Globe at Tiger Mart or at the Circle K store just east of Globe on U.S. Route 70.

288 Salt River Canyon — You are about to enter the deep gorge of the Salt River Canyon, occasionally called "the Grand Canyon you can drive into." The Salt River got its name from the salty taste it has after it flows past salt deposits 15 miles downstream.

While the highway drops steeply, the roadway is wide and well-engineered. Nevertheless, check your brakes before making the descent. Before reaching the next milepost, you will have some excellent views of the canyon and the meandering green stripe of the Salt River at its bottom.

Until this road was built in the early 1930s, travel from the White Mountains to Phoenix usually took two or three days — and numerous tires.

290 Scenic Overlook — You are approaching a scenic pullout on the left side of the highway. Use caution when turning across the oncoming lane. Just before reaching Milepost 291 there is another pullout on the right side of the highway for easier and safer access to a bird's-eye view of the canyon.

293 Picnic Area — Just before reaching Milepost 293, you will arrive at a scenic point near the Salt River bridge. This one has picnic tables and a set of steps that lead down to the river's edge. If you enjoy exploring, there is a dirt road at the bottom of the canyon (generally suitable for passenger autos) that provides a scenic, but sometimes bumpy drive along the river.

297 Looking Back — As you climb out of the canyon, there is yet another vista point and parking area beyond Milepost 297. On the far side of the canyon is Becker's Butte, an imposing formation of redwall limestone named after early-day merchant, trailblazer, and road builder Gustav Becker, who had a farm in Springerville.

311 Cibecue — After this milepost, Apache Route 12, a paved road, leads 14 miles west to the small Indian community of Cibecue. In 1881, six cavalry men and one Apache medicine man were killed in a skirmish here. When the cavalry commander asked an Apache scout what they called the place, the scout told him *she-be-ku,* "my house." The area provides pleasant campsites and good fishing for rainbow and brown trout in nearby Cibecue Creek. A tribal permit is required and may be purchased at the store near the Salt River Canyon bridge (18 miles south on U.S. 60 near Milepost 293).

318 **Carrizo** — The name of the junction near this milepost means "cat-tails." Nearby Carrizo Creek runs into the Salt River. From this point, State Route 73 heads east 23 miles to the town of Fort Apache. Some of the fort's original buildings are still standing. General Crook's log cabin is one. There is also a small museum. Another few miles brings you to Whiteriver, the reservation's administrative headquarters and largest town.

328 **Corduroy Canyon** — You are about to cross Corduroy Canyon. The name is derived from the fact that, in 1880, soldiers from nearby Fort Apache built a road to Show Low. Where it followed the stream the road was made of logs (a corduroy road). Nature claimed the logs and the road long ago, but the name remained.

336 **Apache-Sitgreaves National Forest** — Beyond this milepost you leave the reservation and enter Apache-Sitgreaves National Forest. You have also topped out above the Mogollon Rim and are now on the vast, uplifted landmass of the Colorado Plateau, which extends across northeastern Arizona and beyond the borders of Utah, New Mexico, and Colorado.

339 **State Route 260 West** — Beyond this milepost State Route 260 leads westward to Heber, Payson, and the high country along the Mogollon Rim. It makes an interesting alternate route for a return trip to southern Arizona. (See page 155.)

340 **Show Low** — You are now entering the business and residential areas of Show Low, a pine-country community that has grown markedly in recent decades to serve visitors to Arizona's

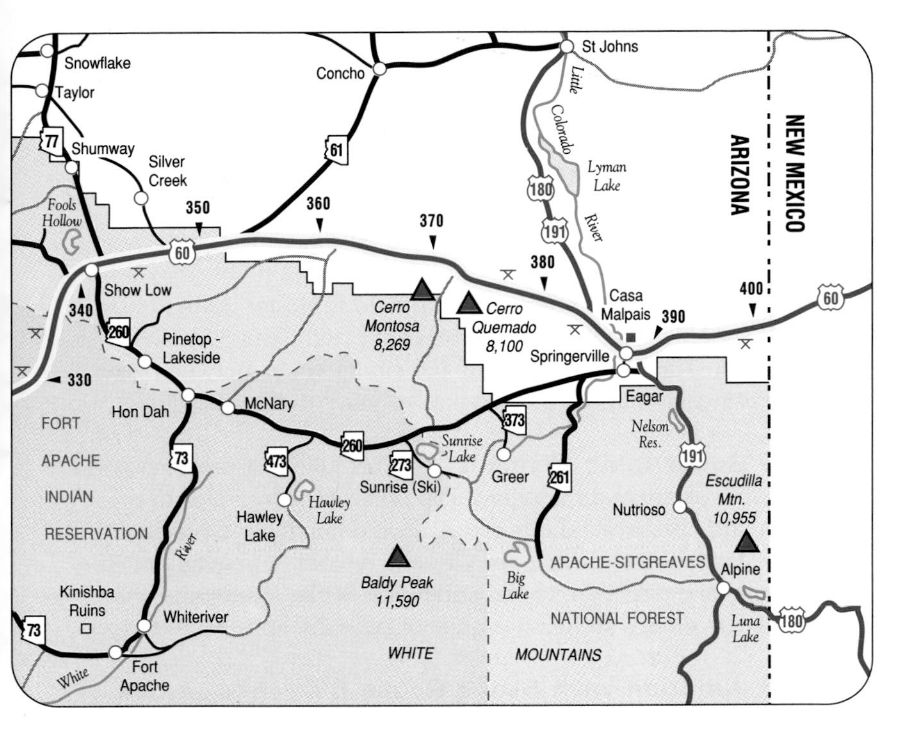

popular White Mountain country. The name is taken from a winner-take-all card game that determined ownership of the land now occupied by the community.

In 1872-73 Corydon Cooley was a scout for George Crook on his campaigns through this area. Upon leaving the army, about 1875, Cooley and Marion Clark started a ranch here. The men began to feel there wasn't enough room for both of them and decided to settle the matter with a game of cards. On the final hand Clark said "show low and you win." Corydon Cooley showed the two of clubs and walked away with nearly 100,000 acres of land.

341 Junction with State Route 260 — Route 260 angles southeast through Pinetop-Lakeside to the very heart of the White Mountains. Lakes, trout streams, and the Sunrise Ski Resort are accessed by this route.

342 State Route 77 — This route runs north through Snowflake to Holbrook, Petrified Forest National Park, and the vastness of the Navajo and Hopi Indian reservations.

344 White Mountain Volcanic Field — To the south rises a bright red cinder cone (a small ancient volcano) with much of its material quarried and hauled away for road building. You are now surrounded by the White Mountain volcanic field. The most prominent volcano in the field is Mount Baldy (clearly visible at Milepost 383), an 11,590-foot peak about 35 miles southeast. There are more than 200 cinder cones between your present position and Springerville, 40 miles to the east.

350 Geographic Diversity — This milepost presents good evidence of Arizona's geographical diversity. Fifty miles to the north and just below the horizon are the multicolored formations of the Painted Desert that are virtually devoid of vegetation. In the opposite direction, to the south, the White Mountains are thickly covered with heavy stands of pine, fir, spruce, and aspen.

352 Junction with State Route 61 — You are now leaving Navajo County and entering Apache County. Just ahead is the junction of State Route 61, a paved highway that leads to Concho, St. Johns, and north to the Petrified Forest National Park (a distance of 44 miles).

367 Cinder Cones — South of the highway at a 1 o'clock position is the impressive bulk of Cerro Montosa, a cinder cone that reaches an elevation of 8,268 feet. Because it is mostly compacted volcanic cinders, the peak supports only sparse plant growth. Farther to the east, Cerro Quemado (8,100 feet) is an even more barren cinder cone.

372 Back Road to Sunrise — For those with a desire to explore the back country, a dirt road heads south just beyond this milepost to intersect with State Route 260 in the vicinity of the Sunrise Ski Resort. Use caution in wet weather and avoid this road entirely during winter months.

378 Escudilla Mountain — At a 1 o'clock position, and outlined against the sky, is Escudilla Mountain, a rather flat-topped peak that is Arizona's third-highest (elevation of 10,955 feet). Located approximately 25 miles south of Springerville on U.S. Route 666, the Escudilla Wilderness offers a hiking trail to the highest lookout tower in Arizona. The area is densely forested and is home to black bear, elk, deer, and many species of smaller animals. For information on the Escudilla Wilderness, and other White Mountain areas, inquire at the U.S. Forest Service offices on South Mountain Avenue near downtown Springerville.

383 Mount Baldy — For a distant view of Mount Baldy, Arizona's second highest peak at 11,500 feet, look to the south. Standing against the horizon, this ancient volcano (8 to 9 million years old) is sacred ground to the Apache Indians; therefore, much of the area near the summit is off-limits, except to tribal members. Even in warmer months, snow is frequently visible on its uppermost slopes.

384 Junction with U.S. Route 191 — Beyond this milepost U.S. Route 191 heads north to St. Johns, which is the Apache County seat. The town dates back to 1872 when it was settled by Mexican-Americans who built a bridge across the Little Colorado River. They originally called the town El Vadito, "little crossing," but, later, in celebration of St. John's Day (June 24), the name was changed. Mormons began colonizing the area in 1880.

386 The Little Colorado River — Beyond this milepost a bridge crosses the Little Colorado River. This small stream flows more than 200 miles in a northwesterly direction to join the mighty Colorado River in the upper reaches of the Grand Canyon. It is difficult to imagine that a 30-minute drive to the south brings you to the type of country pictured below, where streams are fed by melting snow and springs in the high mountains.

387 Casa Malpais Archeological Site — Nestled into a cliff face about 2 miles off the highway, Casa Malpais promises to become one of Arizona's premier archeological sites. Built around A.D. 1250, this prehistoric community of the Mogollon culture features the ruins of a masonry pueblo, a great kiva, fortified walls, and underground ceremonial chambers in a series of caverns. For information on touring the site, inquire at the Casa Malpais Museum in downtown Springerville.

388 Springerville — In 1875, Henry Springer came here from Albuquerque and set up a general store. Unfortunately he extended credit to horse thieves and outlaws and soon went broke. The next year, brothers Julius and Gustav Becker freighted in supplies for a store. Nevertheless, when it came time to name the post office of the growing settlement, someone jokingly suggested Springerville, and the name stuck.

Julius W. Becker, Gustav's son, was instrumental in establishing the first highway through Springerville in 1910. It is in recognition of those first pioneers and transcontinental travelers that Springerville erected the imposing 18-foot-tall statue of the Madonna of the Trail near the center of town.

Springerville today serves the ranching and lumbering industries as well as tourists who come to explore White Mountain country.

If you are continuing on to New Mexico, you will be crossing the state line in about 25 miles.

INDEX

Text (light face)	184
Photo (red bold face)	**184**
Map reference	181m

Saguaro forest, Saguaro National Monument West, Tucson, Arizona. JAMES TALLON

Don't miss these other great travel books from *Arizona Highways*.

Travel Arizona — This best-selling full-color guide leads the way to the state's most popular attractions with 16 motor tours. 128 pages. Softcover. #TABS0 $9.95

Travel Arizona: The Back Roads — Travel 20 backroad tours from desert to highlands to canyons. 136 pages. Softcover. #TBRS9 $9.95

Arizona Road Atlas — Revised to help you find your way around the state with 17 regional maps and maps of 27 cities. 56 pages. Softcover. #ARAS2 $4.95

Scenic Sedona — Explore the incomparable red rock scenery, rich history, and culture of Sedona and the Verde Valley. 64 pages. Softcover. #SSSS1 $5.95

Arizona's Mogollon Rim — Tour Arizona's forested highland plateau dotted by trout-filled lakes and crossed by miles of wilderness hiking trails. 64 pages. Softcover. #AMRS2 $8.50

Arizona Travel Map — Photographs of Arizona's national parks and monuments, and a descriptive list of scenic points of interest, make this the perfect traveling companion. #MAPAZ3 $1.00

OUTDOORS IN ARIZONA SERIES:

A Guide to Hiking and Backpacking — An insiders guide to Arizona's back country featuring 48 hikes through mountains, canyons, forests, and deserts. 136 pages. Softcover. #OHKS7 $9.95

A Guide to Camping — All the information you'll need for your next camping adventure. Features hundreds of campsites throughout the state. 128 pages. Softcover. #OCPS6 $9.95

A Guide to Fishing and Hunting — A variety of Arizona's finest fishing holes and hunting grounds. 180 full-color photographs and helpful maps. 192 pages. Softcover. #OFHS5 $9.95

To order the above *Arizona Highways* books, or to get a free catalog describing other products, write:

Arizona Highways
2039 West Lewis Avenue
Phoenix, Arizona 85009

Or call toll-free nationwide, 1-800-543-5432.
In the Phoenix area, call 602-258-1000.

Shipping and handling charges will be added to your order.
Prices and product availability subject to change.